Pan Study

Biology

N. P. O. Green, J. M. Potter, G. W. Stout

Pan Books London and Sydney
in association with **Heinemann Educational Books**

First published 1980 by Pan Books Ltd,
Cavaye Place, London SW10 9PG
in association with Heinemann Educational Books Ltd
9
ISBN 0 330 25971 7
© N. P. O. Green, J. M. Potter, G. W. Stout
Printed and bound in Great Britain by
Richard Clay (The Chaucer Press) Ltd, Bungay, Suffolk

This book is sold subject to the condition that it
shall not, by way of trade or otherwise, be lent, re-sold,
hired out, or otherwise circulated without the publisher's prior
consent in any form of binding or cover other than that in which
it is published and without a similar condition including this
condition being imposed on the subsequent purchaser

PAN STUDY AIDS

Titles published in this series

Accounts and Book-keeping
Biology
British Government and Politics
Chemistry
Commerce
Economics
Effective Study Skills
English Language
French
Geography 1   *Physical and Human*
Geography 2   *British Isles, Western Europe, North America*
German
History 1   *British*
History 2   *European*
Human Biology
Maths
Physics
Sociology
Spanish

Brodies Notes on English Literature

This long established series published in Pan Study Aids now contains more than 150 titles. Each volume contains one of the major works of English literature regularly set for examinations.

Contents

Acknowledgements 4

To the student 5

1 Guide to revision 7

2 The cell and organization of Life 13

3 Nutrition 38

4 Respiration 63

5 Transport 85

6 Excretion, osmoregulation and temperature regulation 103

7 Coordination 120

8 Skeleton and locomotion 145

9 Reproduction, growth and development 157

10 Genetics and evolution 184

11 Ecology and microbiology 200

12 Guide to examinations 221

Acknowledgements

The publishers are grateful to the following Exam Boards, whose addresses are listed on page 229, for permission to reproduce questions from examination papers:

Associated Examination Board, University of Cambridge Local Examinations Syndicate, Joint Matriculation Board, University of London Schools Examination Board, Northern Ireland Schools Examination Council, Oxford Delegacy of Local Examinations, Oxford and Cambridge Schools Examination Board, Scottish Certificate of Education Examining Board, Southern University Joint Board, Welsh Joint Education Committee.

To the student

The aim of this book is to provide a straightforward guide to study and revision in O level biology. It is not intended to replace a textbook or your own notes. It is written simply, in order to focus your revision onto the main points required to produce sound, biologically correct answers.

A great many examination candidates at O level obtain either Grade C or Grade D. For these people every additional mark is vital to success. Many students receive little instruction in how to study, revise and tackle examination questions, and often are not even sure which are the important facts within the topics they have studied. If you are such a candidate, this book is written with you in mind.

Examinations are designed to test your knowledge and understanding of a subject. A variety of types of questions may be used in examinations, e.g. essay, practical, short answer and multiple choice. You must be thoroughly familiar with the question types used by your examination board. Each will test your ability to:

1 recall facts, principles and concepts given in the syllabus;
2 comment on biological observations and experiments;
3 apply previous knowledge to new situations;
4 analyse and interpret data to produce a conclusion.

The examination syllabuses are designed to encourage an understanding of basic biological principles and facts are used to illustrate them. In revision you are expected to understand the principles and learn and memorize the facts. For example, the detailed facts concerning nutrition in *Amoeba*, a mammal, a parasite, a saprophyte and a flowering plant may all be used to illustrate the principle that 'all living cells require food'.

It is suggested that this book is used in conjunction with your notes throughout your revision and that you should begin by reading the first chapter which gives advice on how to revise.

Each chapter deals with a specific topic for revision. Some questions may require knowledge from several topics and this should not be forgotten. The chapters have four sections:

1 definitions;
2 basic information required by the syllabuses, incorporating past questions;

3 key words;
4 questions from past papers for you to think about (the content of the answers to these questions will be found in the chapter).

How to look up a reference

At the end of each chapter is a list of important biological terms arranged in the order in which they appear in the chapter.
1 Select the chapter according to the topic you are studying, and turn to the list of key words at the end.
2 Find the term you wish to refer to and look it up in the chapter, where it will appear in **bold print.**
3 In doing this you will notice how it relates to the topic as a whole. This should increase the effectiveness of your learning and prepararation for the examination.

In the preparation of this guide the syllabuses of the following examination boards were consulted:

Associated Examining Board (AEB)
Joint Matriculation Board (JMB)
Northern Ireland Examination Board (NI)
Oxford and Cambridge Schools Examining Board (O & C)
Oxford Delegacy of Local Examinations (O)
Scottish Certificate of Education Examination Board (SCE)
Southern Universities Joint Board for Examinations (SU)
University of Cambridge Local Examinations Syndicate (CAM)
University of London School Examination Board (LOND)
Welsh Joint Education Committee (W)

1 Guide to revision

To do well in examinations requires more than good luck. In fact, good candidates eliminate luck from the examination by adequate revision.

Your revision should be so complete that you are able to walk into the examination and know that, whatever topics come up and however the questions are worded, you will be able to answer them satisfactorily. It is important not to be overconfident but your revision should remove all panic and fright from examinations. There is only one way to guarantee success and that is by your own determination and hard work.

Ideally, revision should be a continuing process that begins when you start an examination course. Each topic should be revised as it is covered and questions answered and corrected at all stages. Term and end-of-year examinations should continue to provide familiarity with the subject and examination technique.

However, revision for the vast majority of students is a once only event prior to examinations. With this in mind the following is a suggested approach to your revision. Remember that revision, like living organisms, requires a continual input of energy in order to be successful. The fuel in this case is hard work.

Timing
Give yourself plenty of time to avoid last-minute panic and late nights. Aim at having completed all your revision by the date of your first examination. After this date your time will be required for keeping the facts fresh in your mind.

Organization
1 Find out the dates of your exams and the form of each paper in terms of topic areas and style of questions.
2 Obtain a syllabus and recent examination papers. This is not essential but some students gain confidence from a familiarity with both.

3 Work out a programme of revision in terms of subjects and topics within them and keep to it. This is the sort of discipline needed for revision.
4 Ensure that your school or college notes are complete. All the information required for your revision should be in your notebooks and not in the textbook. Try to avoid having to use this for revision. From now on use it only as a reference book – it has done its job.
5 Tidy up your files or notebooks so that they are a pleasure to revise from.

In carrying out the above you have successfully begun your revision.

Revision technique

The use of multiple-choice questions and compulsory short answers means that questions can be set covering the whole of the syllabus. Therefore you must have a thorough knowledge of all of the syllabus.

Your method of revision is something which is personal but you may find this method helpful.

1 Revise the course topic by topic using the headings given in the contents of this book.
2 Read through your notes on a topic and make a list of sub-topics, e.g.

> *Topic*   – eye
> *Sub-topics* – structure
>   function of parts
>   accommodation
>   sight defects and treatment
>   colour vision
>   binocular vision

(Use the relevant chapter in the revision guide to help you with this.) Take each one in turn and read through it several times. Make a list of the key facts involved in the structure or function being studied and check your understanding of all the biological terms and definitions. Try to identify the principles which appear.
3 Any tables which appear should be thoroughly studied and the details learned. A useful way of memorizing tabulated information is by the use of a **mnemonic** (nem-on-ic). This involves arranging the facts so that their first letters spell out a word.

For example, the characteristics of all living organisms are:

Movement, Assimilation, Respiration, Reproduction, Irritability, Growth, Excretion, which spells out (phonetically) **marri(a)ge**.

An alternative way is to make up a short phrase where the first letter of each word uses the same first letter as those in the list. For example, a useful mnemonic to help remember the order of enzymes involved in mammalian digestion is '**A**rsenic **p**oisoning **r**arely **a**ffects **t**he **l**ittle **m**ice **l**iving **e**ternally **i**n **p**eace'.

These first letters stand for:

amylase	trypsinogen	enterokinase
pepsin	lipase	invertase
rennin	maltase	peptidases
amylase	lactase	

4 The only satisfactory way to learn a diagram is to draw it several times. Simplify diagrams as much as possible so you can draw and label them in 3–4 minutes. For complex diagrams such as organs or organ systems you should be able to draw two diagrams:

(*a*) a labelled sketch diagram showing structures and functions. This may be used to illustrate a point in an essay answer (*see* Fig. 5.3.)
(*b*) a fully labelled and accurately proportioned diagram. This may be demanded by the question and time is allowed to draw this, e.g. '*Draw a labelled diagram of the mammalian heart showing the direction of blood flow.*' (*See* Fig. 5.4.)

All diagrams should be large, labelled and drawn in pencil. Shading should not be used and the use of coloured pencils should be restricted to blood vessels. Each diagram or drawing should have a reference (which may be used elsewhere in the answer) and a title, e.g.

Fig. 5.3 Structure of the human heart

5 Read through the appropriate chapter in the revision guide and check your list to be sure that all points have been covered and are understood. Remember that the guide contains the minimum information considered necessary to obtain a good pass. The key words for each chapter list all the biological terms which are likely to appear on the examiner's mark sheet. Use them as a check list during revision and be sure that you understand them and can use them correctly in your answers.

6 As an aid to learning construct your own revision flow diagrams. This is a useful technique in revision and examinations since it is a good way to plan answers to essay questions and it shows the interrelationships which exist between topics. (Examiners use this technique in setting questions and preparing mark schemes.)

To construct a flow diagram you take a sheet of paper and lay out the main points allowing plenty of space around each. Using these points to suggest other words to you (stimuli) build up the diagram, linking the words with lines and arrows to show functional relationships. In the example given below (*see* Fig. 1.1.) the three main points involved in gas exchange in a mammal were listed as

> **atmosphere** – the source of oxygen
> **lungs** – the gas exchange organ
> **tissues** – the source of carbon dioxide

Other terms were added, where appropriate, using the main points as stimuli. You can add further information to Fig. 1.1. to convert it

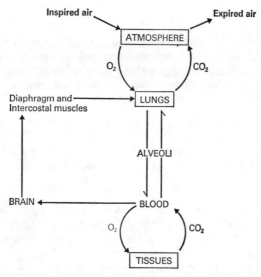

Fig. 1.1 Flow diagram of gas exchanges in the mammal

into a more complete revision aid as shown in Fig. 1.2:

Guide to revision 11

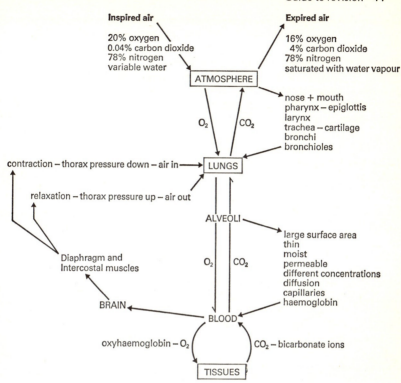

Fig. 1.2 Revision flow diagram of gas exchanges in the mammal

The value of these diagrams in revision lies in the fact that they are constructed by you. Their structure is unique and means something to you. It is important that they should include all the key points and that each word you write down should act as a stimulus for another word. The construction of these diagrams is one of the most efficient ways of recalling facts. Research into the processes of memory and recall have shown that detailed material is best conserved in memory if first represented in simplified ways.

Try this out for yourself and construct a flow diagram for the structure of the mammalian alimentary canal starting with the key words mouth, stomach, intestine, anus. You may be surprised by how much detail you can add. Remember to keep your diagrams simple.

7 Read chapter 12 (p221) and take note of all the advice given on how to understand the variety of questions and how to prepare answers to them.
8 Having revised a topic as suggested, the next step is to look at the past questions given in the guide. Now try answering some of the questions which have been set on previous papers. The questions given in the guide cover those topics which tend to crop up most frequently in examinations.

At first take your time and use references, but later you must practise answering questions without references and in the time allowed in the examination. Always have your answers marked.

2 The cell and organization of life

Protoplasm The material of which all living cells are made.
Cell A unit of protoplasm having a single nucleus and cytoplasm surrounded by a cell membrane.
Nucleus A denser area within a cell surrounded by a nuclear membrane, and containing the hereditary material.
Cytoplasm The protoplasm of a cell, excluding the nucleus, composed mainly of organelles.
Plasmalemma Membrane surrounding the protoplasm of the cell.
Organelle A specialized structure within the cell, e.g. nucleus.
Tissue A group of similar cells performing the same function more efficiently than they would alone, e.g. muscle.
Organ A structure formed by two or more tissues working together to perform particular functions, e.g. stomach.
Organism A single individual of a species.
Diffusion The movement of molecules from a region of their high concentration to one of their low concentration.
Osmosis The movement of *water* molecules from a region of their high concentration to one of their low concentration through a partially permeable (semi-permeable) membrane.
Active transport The movement of substances from a region of their low concentration to one of their high concentration. This movement requires energy.
Enzyme A protein molecule, produced by living cells to catalyse a chemical reaction.

Characteristics of living organisms

All living organisms are made of **protoplasm** which shows characteristics not displayed by similar non-living organic material. All living organisms show some or all of these characteristics.

1 **Movement** A change in position of the whole body, part of the body, or within a cell, using energy produced by the organism (*see* chapters 5, 7, 8).

2 **Assimilation and nutrition** All living organisms need a supply of nourishment to maintain the structure of the body and to provide energy (*see* chapter 2).

3 **Respiration** The process by which energy is liberated in cells by the breakdown of food materials (*see* chapter 4).

4 **Reproduction** The production of other individuals of the same species (*see* chapter 9).

5 **Irritability** The ability to respond to a stimulus (*see* chapter 7).

6 **Growth** An increase in the amount of living material in an organism produced from substances unlike itself (*see* chapter 9).

7 **Excretion** The removal from the body of the waste products produced by chemical processes in the cells (*see* chapter 6).

Protoplasm shows certain similarities wherever it is found. It is composed of:

1 Water, which is a vital constituent making up 80–90% of its weight. It contains dissolved mineral salts, e.g. chlorides, phosphates, bicarbonates, sulphates, nitrates, of sodium, potassium, magnesium and calcium; and food materials, e.g. sugars, fats and amino acids.
2 A protein framework, in which the protein forms a colloidal suspension in water. This has certain properties including the ability to change between liquid (sol) and semi-solid (gel) states (*ref.* movement in *Amoeba*, p17).
3 The framework supports and separates the enzyme systems responsible for all the chemical processes of the protoplasm.
4 Protoplasm forms organelles which perform specific functions within the cell. The unit of which most organelles are formed is a membrane

composed of two layers of fat molecules sandwiched between two layers of protein molecules.

Levels of organization

Living systems function at several levels showing increasing complexity and organization. Each level is built up from the levels below:

atomic → molecular → organelle → cell → tissue → organ
↓
community ← population ← organism ← organ system
↓
ecosystem

The structures and functions which constitute life rely on about twenty different elements, e.g. hydrogen, carbon, oxygen, nitrogen.

Atoms of these elements are arranged to make molecules, e.g. carbohydrates, amino acids, fats, and these form the basis of all other levels.

Cell structure
Animal and plant cells have the following basic structure.

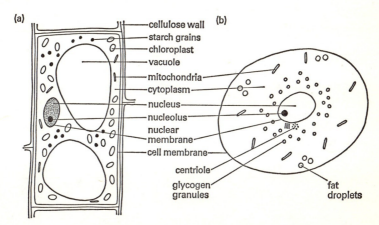

Fig. 2.1 (a) Typical plant cell, (b) typical animal cell

Far more detail can be seen in cells using the electron microscope.

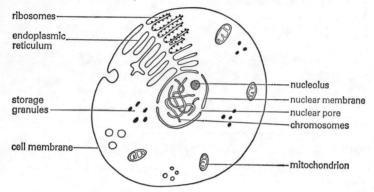

Fig. 2.2 Generalized cell seen under electron microscope

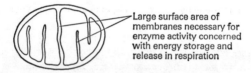

Fig. 2.3 Mitochondrion

Endoplasmic reticulum An extensive system of membranes extending through the cytoplasm and giving enormous surface area for exchange between cell and environment.

Ribosomes Small bodies made of ribonucleic acid, usually situated on the endoplasmic reticulum, whose function is protein synthesis.

Plasmalemma The cell membrane which controls the passage of substances in and out of cell.

Nuclear membrane Surrounds nucleus and is continuous with endoplasmic reticulum. Has nuclear pores through which communication between nucleus and cytoplasm can take place.

Chromosomes Structures within the nucleus carrying the information for building cell, and responsible for passing on hereditary factors.

The cell and organization of life 17

Table 1.1 Differences between plant and animal cells

Plant cell	Animal cell
Cell wall	No rigid wall
No centrioles	Centrioles present
Large permanent vacuoles of cell sap	Vacuoles small and temporary
Storage – starch and protein	Storage – glycogen and fat
Chloroplasts often present	Chloroplasts not present

Table 1.2 Differences between plants and animals

Plants	Animals
Holophytic nutrition – chlorophyll	Holozoic nutrition – no chlorophyll
Non-motile	Motile
Growth at stem and root tips ; goes on throughout life of plant	Growth all over body ; stops when adult size reached
Branched – large surface area for exchange	Compact for movement
Slow reactions controlled by hormones	Rapid reactions – nervous system

Some microscopic organisms exist as a single cell and all the functions of life occur within a single unit of protoplasm, e.g. *Amoeba*.

A simple animal – Amoeba

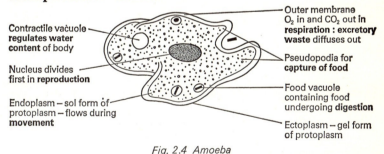

Fig. 2.4 Amoeba

The whole animal reacts to touch and the presence of food – shows irritability. Increase of protoplasm through nutrition produces growth.

In larger animals and plants the body is divided into a number of cells which act as a unit and also as part of the whole body. Sometimes these cells are all similar and perform all living functions, e.g. *Spirogyra*.

A simple plant – Spirogyra

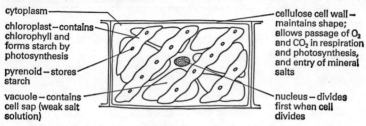

Fig. 2.5 Spirogyra

A multicellular organism – *Hydra*

In multicellular organisms, e.g. *Hydra*, cells undergo **differentiation** and their structure becomes specialized to enable them to carry out fewer functions more efficiently. This process can lead to division of labour. These cells cannot exist independently and only function as part of the organism.

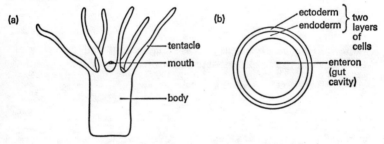

Fig. 2.6 (a) Hydra, (b) transverse section through body

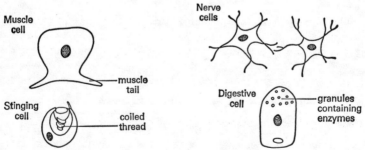

Fig. 2.7 Cell types in Hydra to show differentiation

Tissue structure

A number of similar cells working together is called a **tissue**, and is more efficient than scattered cells working separately. The main tissues are epithelial, connective (blood, lymph, bone), muscular and nervous. Examples of muscle and bone cells are given in Figs. 2.8 and 2.9. In

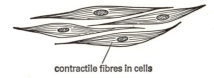

Fig. 2.8 Muscle cells from the intestine (these contract to cause movement)

more complex animals and plants, **organs** are formed by the combination of a number of tissues and these may be grouped into **organ systems** which are responsible for various functions within the organism, e.g. heart, blood vessels and blood form the circulatory system.

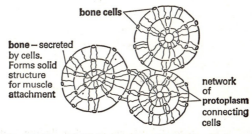

Fig. 2.9 Bone cells (these support muscle attachment)

The inter-relationships between the structure and function of tissues, organs and organ systems are clearly seen in the most advanced plants, e.g. the Angiosperms (flowering plants).

Structure and function of the flowering plant

Flowering plants are composed of the cell types shown in Table 1.3.

Table 1.3 Plant cell types

Region	Tissue	Structure Wall	Contents	Function
Epidermis	**Epidermal**	Cellulose, thick with cuticle	Living	Protection
Cortex and pith	**Parenchyma**	Cellulose, thin	Living	Support by turgor
	Chlorenchyma	Cellulose, thin	Living	Some photosynthesis
Cortex	**Collenchyma**	Cellulose, thickened at corners	Living	Support
Cortex, vascular bundles	**Sclerenchyma (fibres)**	Lignin, thickened	Dead	Support
Vascular bundles	**Xylem**	Lignin, thickened, no end walls	Dead	Water and salt transport, support
	Cambium	Cellulose, very thin	Living	Cell division
	Phloem (sieve tube)	Cellulose, thickened, perforated end walls (sieve plates)	Dead	Translocation of sugars and amino acids
	(companion cell)	Cellulose, thin	Living	
Cortex in old stem and root	**Cork**	Suberin, thickened	Dead	Protection against desiccation

Table 1.3 may look formidable but easy marks can be picked up by having a thorough knowledge of it, e.g.

For each of the descriptions A–D select the appropriate items from the list 1–6

<table>
<tr><td>A</td><td>conducts sugars</td><td>1</td><td>root hair cell</td></tr>
<tr><td>B</td><td>has lignified (woody) walls</td><td>2</td><td>xylem</td></tr>
<tr><td>C</td><td>forms the outer covering of a young stem</td><td>3</td><td>epidermis</td></tr>
<tr><td>D</td><td>is capable of dividing</td><td>4</td><td>cambium</td></tr>
<tr><td></td><td></td><td>5</td><td>phloem</td></tr>
<tr><td></td><td></td><td>6</td><td>guard cell (JMB)</td></tr>
</table>

Examples of cell types

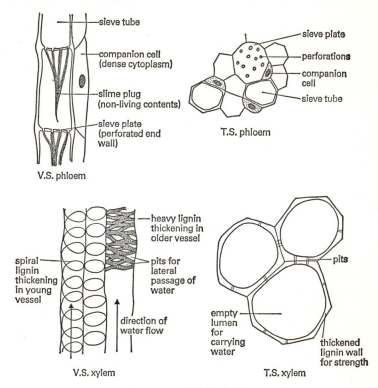

Fig. 2.10 Vascular tissues

These tissues are grouped together to form the organs, root, stem, leaf and flower. Finally these are arranged to form the two organ systems, the root system (below ground) and the shoot system (above ground), of the organism.

Root system
The functions of this system are anchorage and the absorption of water and minerals.

External features The primary root develops from the **radicle** of the seed. It usually grows vertically downwards (positive geotropism, *see* p124). Secondary roots branch from the primary and spread out sideways, giving anchorage and drawing water and mineral salts from a large volume of soil.

The tip of each branch of the root is covered by a protective **root cap** from which cells are continually worn away by friction and replaced by new cells from the growing point.

Just behind the tip of each root is a region bearing numerous delicate **root hairs**. These die as the root grows on, and are replaced by new ones, so that a band of hairs always exists at the same distance behind the root tip.

Each hair is an elongated epidermal cell with a *thin* cellulose wall. It is in close contact with the soil particles. The root hairs give a very large surface area for the absorption of water and salts.

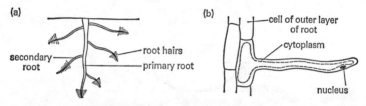

Fig. 2.11 (a) Tap root, (b) root hair cell

Internal structure Growth occurs as a result of the activity of the **apical meristem** (growing point) at each root tip. Cells produced here elongate by absorption of water, and then become differentiated into tissues with different functions (*see* Fig. 2.12).

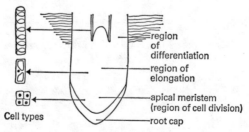

Fig. 2.12 V.S. root tip

The **vascular** or conducting tissue of the root forms a central core called the **stele** (Fig. 2.13). The **xylem** which conducts water, also provides mechanical strength. This arrangement gives the root strength to resist the pulling strains which result from movement of the aerial part of the plant.

The xylem is arranged in the shape of a star alternating with the **phloem**. A well-defined **endodermis** surrounds the vascular tissue. A wide **cortex**, which often contains storage tissue, separates the stele from the outer **exodermis**, which in a young root will bear root hairs. Roots are sometimes specialized for storage, e.g. **tap root** (carrot), **root tuber** (dahlia).

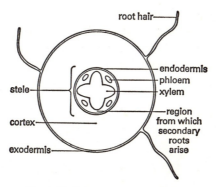

Fig. 2.13 T.S. primary root of bean

Shoot system
The functions of this system are the support of leaves in light and air, and of flowers and fruit for sexual reproduction.

External features The main shoot develops from the **plumule** of the seed. It usually bears a **terminal bud** at the tip by which increase in length takes place. Lateral or **axillary buds** in leaf axils produce side branches. Flowers and fruits appear at certain times of the year. Regions of the stem where leaves are produced are called **nodes**. Those parts of the stem between the nodes are **internodes** (*see* Fig. 2.14).

Young stems are usually green because the outer tissues contain chloroplasts. The surface of all the aerial parts of the plant is covered by a waterproof cuticle or later by cork to prevent loss of water.

The general shape of the aerial part of the plant is formed by the reactions of the stem to gravity and light. The main stem grows vertically upwards away from gravity, and all stems grow towards light.

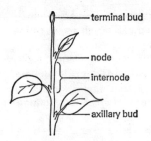

Fig. 2.14 Shoot system

Internal structure A single ring of **vascular bundles** lies near the outside of the stem. Each bundle contains xylem and phloem separated by a narrow band of **cambium**. Cell division in the cambium increases

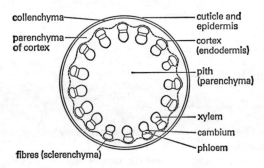

Fig. 2.15 T.S. young stem of sunflower

the amount of the other tissues. In most plants **fibres** give additional strength (*see* Fig. 2.15). The vascular bundles are important because they:

1 carry water and salts (xylem);
2 carry sugars and amino acids (phloem);
3 give support to the stem (xylem and fibres).

Central to the bundles are the turgid **parenchyma** cells of the **pith** which provide support for the stem.

Outside the bundles lies a narrow **cortex**. The inner part of this is made up of parenchyma cells which may contain storage starch grains. The outer part may be **collenchyma** giving strength to the outer layers of the stem (with its thickened cellulose walls). These outer cells which receive light may contain chloroplasts enabling photosynthesis to take place (chlorenchyma).

On the outside of the stem is a single layer of cells called the **epidermis**. The cells have thickened walls, and secrete a waterproof **cuticle**.

Questions are often set which require an understanding of the structure and functions of roots and stems. You should use the diagram given and the table below in answering this question.

Draw clearly labelled diagrams of transverse sections of (a) a stem, and (b) a root of a herbaceous dicotyledon. Explain how the structure of stems and roots are suited to their respective functions. [25]   (LOND)

Table 1.4 Structural differences between roots and stems

Roots	Stems
Do not bear buds, leaves or flowers	Bear buds, leaves and flowers
Bear root hairs	Do not bear root hairs
Tip protected by root cap	Tip protected by overlapping leaves
Cambium is not present in young root	Cambium present between xylem and phloem
White or brown	Usually green due to chlorophyll
No cuticle	Outer surface covered with a cuticle
No stomata	Bears stomata in epidermis

Buds

Contain partly developed leaves and sometimes flowers, usually protected by bud scales.

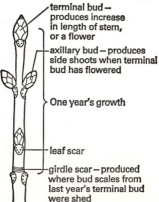

Fig. 2.16 Horse chestnut twig in winter conditions.

Buds are generally dormant in winter and are stimulated to growth in spring. Growth is controlled by chemicals in the plant called hormones which regulate which buds develop when.

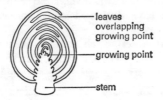

Fig. 2.17 V.S. through large winter bud of Brussels sprout

Leaf

The functions of the leaf are:

1 Photosynthesis (*see* p39)
2 Transpiration (*see* p94)
3 Gas exchange (*see* p80)
4 Protein synthesis (*see* p186)
5 Temporary starch storage (*see* p40).

The **lamina** contains an upper **palisade** tissue of closely packed cells. These cells are rich in **chloroplasts** containing the photosynthetic pigment chlorophyll. The leaf is extended with the upper

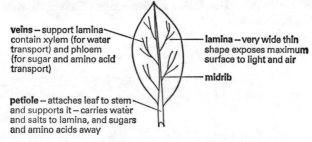

Fig. 2.18 External features of a privet leaf

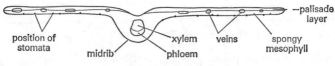

Fig. 2.19 T.S. through lamina

The cell and organization of life 27

surface exposed to light, so that it falls on the palisade layer. Photosynthesis occurs in the chloroplasts. The lower layer of the lamina is the **spongy mesophyll** containing fewer chloroplasts, but many air spaces between the cells. These allow diffusion of gases through the leaf.

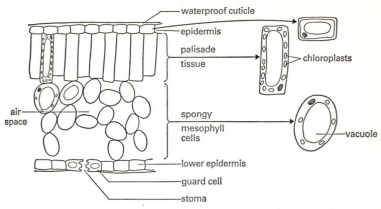

Fig. 2.20 T.S. through privet leaf

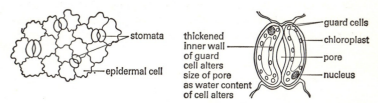

Fig. 2.21 (a) Surface view of lower leaf epidermis; (b) surface view of one stoma, enlarged

The single layer of cells (epidermis) protecting the lamina contains no chloroplasts except in the **guard cells** of the **stomata**. These occur almost entirely in the lower surface of most leaves. Since evaporation of water vapour occurs mainly through the stomata this position away from direct Sun's rays protects the plant from excessive water loss. Oxygen and carbon dioxide diffuse in and out of the leaf through the stomata.

Re-read these notes and study the diagrams to find the information to answer this question. Always qualify each structure with its function.

In what ways are the leaves of plants adapted for photosynthesis? [6]
(O & C)

Physical and chemical features of cells

The importance of water

Life is believed to have originated in the sea. The aquatic environments (marine and freshwater) present fewer problems to living organisms than life on land. All living cells are surrounded by water – it forms their immediate environment.

Water is a vital constituent of all protoplasm and body fluids because:

1 All chemical reactions, secretion, absorption and excretion of substances, occur in solution. Water is the solvent in which substances are dissolved.
2 Transport systems in animals and plants all depend on water as the transport medium, e.g. blood plasma.
3 Water is a raw material of photosynthesis – the main energy-fixing process of living organisms.
4 Loss of water from terrestrial organisms by evaporation and excretion has led to the evolution of many structures and processes to protect them from desiccation, e.g. cuticle in plants, epidermis in mammals.

Exchange of substances between cells and their environment

All living organisms are composed of particles called molecules which are in a state of constant random movement. If the chemical composition of the cells is different from that of their environment, movement of substances in and out of cells will occur. The three processes involved are **diffusion, osmosis** and **active transport.**

A clear understanding of these processes is necessary – it is a popular topic with examiners. Consider the following question when reading these notes.

(a) *What do you understand by the term osmosis?* [5]
(b) *How does diffusion differ from this?* [3]   (O & C)

Diffusion

If the molecules of a liquid, gas or dissolved substance are unevenly distributed in a space, they will by their random movement become evenly distributed. This movement of molecules from an area of their high concentration to one of their low concentration down a concentration gradient is called diffusion.

Any substance which can pass through a cell membrane will diffuse into or out of a cell, in the direction determined by the concentration gradient, e.g. all cells respire and produce carbon dioxide. The concentration of carbon dioxide within the cell rises above that of the environment, and the carbon dioxide diffuses out of the cell.

Osmosis
This is a special type of diffusion. It is the movement of *water* molecules from a region of their high concentration to a region of their low concentration across a partially permeable membrane. It may also be thought of as the passage of water molecules from a weak solution to a strong one, across a semi-permeable membrane.

A membrane which allows the passage of all substances across it is said to be freely permeable. One which prevents the passage of substances across it is said to be impermeable. One which allows water to

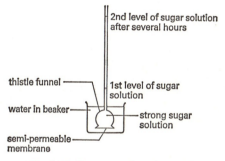

Fig. 2.22 Demonstration of osmosis

pass through but not dissolved substances is partially permeable, e.g. the cell membrane surrounding all cells.

Water can pass through the partially permeable membrane but not the sugar molecules (*see* Fig. 2.22). Because of the higher concentration of water molecules in the beaker more water passes into the thistle funnel than out of it and the level in the tube rises.

The sugar solution is said to have a high **osmotic potential** (osmotic pressure). The water could be replaced by a weak sugar solution, and water would still enter the thistle funnel by osmosis, as long as the sugar solution it contained was stronger (had a higher osmotic pressure or potential).

The osmotic potential (O.P.) of the fluids in cells is related to their

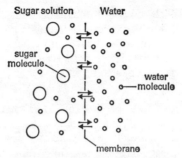

Fig. 2.23 Explanation of osmosis

concentration of dissolved sugars and salts. The cell is surrounded by a semi-permeable cell membrane, so if the fluid outside the cell has a different O.P. from that inside, water will either leave or enter the cell, perhaps with damaging results. Animal cells therefore are either surrounded by body fluids of the same O.P. as themselves, or, as in *Amoeba*, they have a means of adjusting the water content if it changes (*see* p110).

Red blood cells are normally surrounded by a fluid of almost constant osmotic potential, the **plasma**.

If we experimentally surround red blood cells with (a) water and (b) a very strong salt solution, the effect on the cells can be compared with normal cells (c). The arrows in Fig. 2.24 show the water movement.

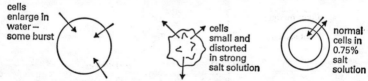

Fig. 2.24 Osmotic effects on red blood cells

Using the information above answer the following question.

When placed in distilled water, red blood corpuscles swell and burst.
  (a) *Explain why the red blood corpuscle swells.*
  (b) *Explain why the red corpuscle bursts.* (AEB)

Plant cells are surrounded by a firm, freely permeable cellulose wall which protects them against bursting if they absorb water (*see* Fig. 2.25 (a)). If however they are put into strong sugar solution water passes out of the cell and it loses its rigidity (*see* Fig. 2.25 (b)). Further water loss causes the cytoplasm to shrink away from the cell wall, and the cell is said to be **plasmolysed** (*see* Fig. 2.25 (c)). **Turgid** cells as in (a) have

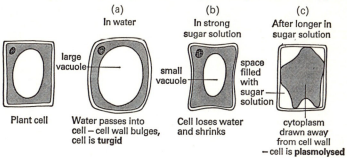

Fig. 2.25 Osmotic effects on plant cells

an important supporting role in herbaceous (non-woody) plants. When all the cells in, e.g. parenchyma tissue, absorb water, each cell swells and presses out against its neighbours. The result is a rigid mass of cells which can support the soft parts of the plant (*see* p154).

Active transport
This is the movement of substances from point A to point B against a concentration gradient and requires energy provided by ATP produced during respiration. It occurs in the movement of substances across the

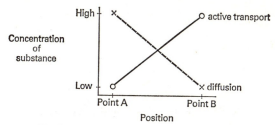

Fig. 2.26 Graph illustrating active transport

cell membrane, either to maintain the constant composition of the cell or to take in raw materials for growth or maintenance of normal functions. **'Carrier'** molecules situated in the cell membrane are thought to be responsible for moving these substances.

Examples
1 The active absorption of mineral salts by the root hair cells of a plant (*see* p99).

2 The completion of the absorption of digested food in the intestine of a mammal (*see* p56).
3 The selective reabsorption of substances back into the blood capillaries in the first convoluted tubule in the kidney (*see* p108).

Food materials in plants and animals

Photosynthesis is the basic process in the production of all food materials in plants. It is the process whereby simple inorganic substances such as carbon dioxide and water are combined to produce complex organic ones (carbohydrates) (*see* chapter 2). From these carbohydrates the leaf forms fats, and by combination with mineral salts it forms proteins and vitamins.

Similar materials found in animals, originate in plants. Animals cannot build up organic materials, and must obtain them from plants or other animals which are themselves dependent on plants.

Carbohydrates These contain the elements carbon, hydrogen, oxygen.

Simple sugars (monosaccharides)	$C_6H_{12}O_6$	Soluble	Glucose, fructose
More complex sugars (disaccharides)	$C_{12}H_{22}O_{11}$	Soluble	Maltose, sucrose
Large molecule carbohydrates (polysaccharides)	$(C_{12}H_{22}O_{11})_n$	Insoluble	Starch, glycogen, cellulose

Carbohydrates formed by photosynthesis are stored as starch in the leaf during the day. At night the starch is hydrolysed (*see* p40) to soluble sugar and translocated to other parts of the plant where it may be stored (as starch) used in the formation of cellulose walls or used in energy production.

In animals, carbohydrate taken in as food is digested to simple sugars by enzymes (*see* p. 33), absorbed and used for energy production or stored as glycogen.

Functions
1 Energy production in cell respiration.
2 Storage as starch in plants, glycogen in animals.
3 Formation of cellulose cell walls.

Fats These contain carbon, hydrogen and oxygen, and are formed by plants from sugars, stored as oil droplets in plant cells and adipose tissue in animals.

Functions
1 Release large amounts of energy when broken down in respiration.
2 Protect internal organs of mammal from damage.
3 Act as a heat insulator in mammal skin.

Proteins These contain carbon, hydrogen, oxygen, nitrogen and sometimes sulphur. They are very large molecules formed of a chain of **amino acids** joined end to end. There are twenty different amino acids which can be joined in any order and any length to make a great variety of different proteins.

Amino acids are formed in the leaf of the green plant by combining sugars with mineral salts (particularly nitrates) absorbed by the root. These amino acids are then combined to form proteins in the ribosomes of the cells (*see* p186).

Functions
1 As an important structural part of protoplasm, and therefore necessary in growth and tissue repair.
2 Formation of enzymes and other functional substances, e.g. haemoglobin, insulin.

Vitamins These are substances vital to life, but only needed in small quantities. They are made by plants. Animals must obtain most of their vitamins from plants because they cannot manufacture their own.

Functions
1 Many vitamins combine with proteins in the formation of enzymes (for special functions *see* p50).

Several simple questions are usually set on the structure and functions of biological molecules. It is a pity to lose easy marks so learn them, e.g.

1 *Of what organic units are proteins composed?* [1]
   Give two functions of proteins in the cells of an organism. [2] (JMB)
2 *What are carbohydrates?* [6] (LOND)

Enzymes
Enzymes are chemical substances which increase the rate of chemical reactions in living organisms or allow them to occur at lower temperatures. The substance acted on by the enzyme is called a **substrate**.

Properties of enzymes
1 Made by living cells.
2 Protein in nature, sometimes incorporating vitamins.
3 Act as catalysts.
4 Responsible for one specific reaction.
5 Can also catalyse the reverse reaction depending on concentration.
6 Rise of temperature increases rate of reaction at low temperatures.
7 Work fastest at a particular temperature (the optimum).
8 Work most efficiently at a particular pH (the optimum).
9 Can be activated by chemicals or other enzymes (e.g. enterokinase activates trypsinogen).
10 Can be inhibited by chemicals (e.g. silver nitrate, cyanide).
11 Destroyed (denatured) by heat (e.g. by boiling).
(For details of enzyme experiments *see* p52.)

Two of the simple reactions vital to life which are **catalysed** by enzymes are **condensation** and **hydrolysis**.

Condensation reactions are involved in the formation of a complex substance from simple ones with the removal of water e.g. synthesis:

$$\text{amino acids} \xrightarrow[\text{condensation}]{\text{enzyme}} \text{protein} + \text{water}$$

Complex insoluble substances are usually used as storage products in cells because they do not produce an osmotic potential and so cause problems of water movement.

Hydrolysis reactions are involved in the splitting of a complex substance into simple substances by the addition of water e.g. digestion:

$$\text{starch} + \text{water} \xrightarrow[\text{hydrolysis}]{\text{enzyme}} \text{sugars}$$

Simple soluble substances are the form in which food materials are translocated (moved around) the body in solution in water. Enzymes are therefore necessary to convert one form into the other.

Complex insoluble substance		Small simple soluble substances		Complex insoluble substance
Plant storage organ	enzymes (hydrolysis) →	*Transport system*	enzymes (condensation) →	*Growing region*

Key words

movement	phloem	spongy mesophyll
assimilation	endodermis	guard cells
respiration	cortex	stomata
reproduction	exodermis	molecules
irritability	tap root	diffusion
growth	root tuber	osmosis
excretion	plumule	partially permeable
protoplasm	terminal bud	membrane
mitochondrion	axil	osmotic pressure
endoplasmic reticulum	axillary bud	osmotic potential
ribosome	node	plasmolysed
plasmalemma	internode	turgid
nuclear membrane	vascular bundle	active transport
chromosomes	cambium	'carrier molecule'
differentiation	fibres	photosynthesis
tissue	parenchyma	carbohydrates
organs	pith	fats
organ systems	cortex	proteins
radicle	collenchyma	amino acids
root cap	epidermis	vitamins
root hair	cuticle	enzymes
apical meristem	buds	substrate
vascular tissue	lamina	catalysts
stele	palisade	condensation
xylem	chloroplasts	hydrolysis

Past examination questions

1 *The action of an enzyme on its substrate at different temperatures was investigated, and the results shown below. Study the graphs and answer the questions that follow.*

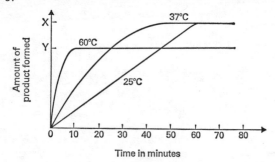

(a) From the graphs, state the time taken before each curve becomes horizontal:
   (i) at 25 °C, (ii) at 37 °C, (iii) at 60 °C.
(b) From the curves shown and your answers in (a), state **one** general deduction that you can make about the effect of temperature upon the rate of enzyme action.
(c) Suggest one reason why the curves labelled 25 °C and 37 °C become level at the same height (X) on the graphs.
(d) Suggest a reason why the horizontal part of the graph labelled 60 °C is at a lower level (Y) than the horizontal parts of the other two curves.
(e) Name **one** enzyme found in plants and another found in animals, stating the substrate upon which each enzyme acts and the products of the reactions.
   (i) in plants, (ii) in animals. (CAM)

Questions 2–7 are concerned with the following parts of the shoot of a flowering plant: A axil, B lenticel, C midrib, D node, E petiole.

Relate each one of the descriptions below with one of the structures above.

2 Where the leaf is attached to the stem.
3 Leaf stalk.
4 Pore in bark through which gases may be exchanged.
5 Main vein of a leaf.
6 Found only in woody stems.
7 Angle between the main stem and leaf stalk. (LOND)

8 Prepare a list of the characteristic features which distinguish a green plant from animals. [5]
What characteristics of plants are also found in animals? [5]

Make labelled drawings of (i) a named plant cell, and (ii) a named animal cell, as seen with the light microscope. [10] (O & C)

9 *In what ways is water essential to the growth of a green plant?* [12] (O & C)

10 *Which one of the following lists of terms are the structures in order of decreasing complexity?*

 A cell, system, organ, tissue, organism
 B organism, system, organ, tissue, cell
 C cell, organ, tissue, system, organism
 D organism, system, tissue, organ, cell
 E organ, system, tissue, cell, organism (JMB)

3 Nutrition

Autotrophic nutrition The nutrition of green plants; the building up of complex organic substances from simple inorganic ones.
Heterotrophic nutrition The taking in of complex organic food materials which are broken down, absorbed and then rebuilt into the animal's protoplasm.
Ingestion The intake of complex organic food into the body.
Digestion The breakdown of large complex insoluble molecules into simple small soluble molecules.
Absorption The uptake of soluble food substances into living cells.
Assimilation The utilization of food substances within the cell.
Egestion The elimination of undigested waste from the body.
Secretion The production of chemical substances by a cell or a gland.
Saprophyte A plant feeding on dead or decaying organic material.
Parasite An organism living in or on another living organism, called the host, from which it obtains food. The parasite may harm the host.

Nutrition supplies:
1 the raw materials for growth, repair and synthesis of essential substances;
2 the fuel from which energy is released to build new tissues, and to perform all essential life processes.

There are two main forms of nutrition, **autotrophic** (holophytic) – typical of green plants, which involves the synthesis of complex substances from simple inorganic ones, and **heterotrophic** nutrition. The latter is further divided into

1 **holozoic** – typical animal nutrition. This involves the processes of **ingestion, digestion** (breakdown of complex organic food), **absorption, assimilation** and **egestion**.

2 **saprophytic** – the nutrition of plants feeding on dead and decaying organic matter.
3 **parasitic** – the nutrition of organisms living in or on a living **host**.

Autotrophic nutrition

Green plants produce carbohydrates by photosynthesis. These can be converted to fats, or by combining with mineral salts, form vitamins and amino acids.

All green parts of the plant which are exposed to light can carry out photosynthesis (*see* p41).

The process can be represented by the following equation:

$$\text{carbon dioxide} + \text{water} \xrightarrow[\text{chlorophyll}]{\text{sunlight}} \text{sugars} + \text{oxygen}$$

$$6CO_2 + 6H_2O \longrightarrow C_6H_{12}O_6 + 6O_2$$

Adequate supplies of the following are necessary for the formation of carbohydrates by photosynthesis: carbon dioxide, water, light and chlorophyll.

Carbon dioxide This is present in the atmosphere in a concentration of 0.04% and enters the leaf by diffusion through the stomata (*see* p82). As it is used up in the leaf cells, a diffusion gradient is set up from the atmosphere to the air spaces of the leaf. Carbon dioxide diffuses through the stomata into the leaf, dissolves in the moisture on the surface of the cells and diffuses to the chloroplasts where photosynthesis takes place. The spongy mesophyll layer has many air spaces to facilitate diffusion (*see* p27).

Water This is absorbed by osmosis through the root hair cells. It passes up in the xylem of root and stem, and out through the veins of the leaf (*see* p96). Use of water in photosynthesis causes more water to be drawn along the veins to the palisade cells.

Light The maximum available light reaches the site of photosynthesis because:

1 leaves on a plant are arranged so that the maximum leaf surface is exposed to the sun (leaf mosaic);
2 the leaf is held at right angles to the direction of the sunlight so that the upper surface receives maximum light;

3 most chloroplasts are in the closely packed upper layer of cells (palisade layer);
4 the chloroplasts in some plants move to the upper parts of the cells in dim light;
5 chlorophyll reflects green light and absorbs red and blue, the wavelengths most valuable in photosynthesis;
6 the enormous surface area/volume ratio of the lamina exposes a very large area of chlorophyll-containing cells to the light.

Use information concerning carbon dioxide, water, light and leaf structure (p27) to answer the following question:

Explain how the leaves of flowering plants are adapted to perform their functions. [7]   (LOND)

Mechanism of reaction

The process of photosynthesis can be divided into two phases:

1 **Light reaction** – chlorophyll absorbs light energy which is converted to chemical energy and used to split water. Oxygen is given off, and the hydrogen is used to reduce carbon dioxide in the second phase.
2 **Dark reaction** – carbon dioxide is reduced by the hydrogen in the presence of enzymes to form simple organic compounds such as **sugars**. This phase is affected by temperature; the light reaction is not.

The following question should help you think out the process of photosynthesis.

Describe fully how sugars are synthesized in a green leaf. [12]   (O)

The sugar is changed to starch immediately, and stored temporarily in the leaf. At night, the starch is hydrolysed by enzymes back to sugar, and carried away in the phloem. It may travel to

1 growing points to be used to provide energy, and in the production of new cell walls;
2 storage organs or seeds, to be redeposited as starch. Starch is stored as starch grains in the cytoplasm of cells, and being insoluble does not set up adverse osmotic pressures in the cells.

Experiments demonstrating photosynthesis

Experiment *To investigate the evolution of oxygen in photosynthesis.*

Apparatus

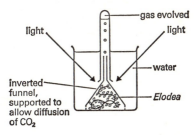

Fig. 3.1

Method *Elodea* was exposed to sunlight for several hours.

Result A gas was evolved which ignited a glowing splint.

Conclusion The gas given off by a green plant in sunlight was oxygen.

Experiment *To investigate the presence of starch in a leaf.*

Method A leaf from a plant which was exposed to sunlight for six hours was detached and (a) dipped into boiling water for 5 minutes to remove the cuticle; (b) boiled in ethyl alcohol to remove the chlorophyll (this is done in a water bath to avoid danger of fire); (c) dipped in boiling water to soften the leaf; (d) spread on a white tile; (e) covered with dilute iodine solution for 1 minute; and (f) washed to remove the iodine solution.

Result and conclusion A blue-black colouration demonstrates the presence of starch. This test is used in experiments to investigate the conditions required for photosynthesis. The presence of starch in a leaf indicates that photosynthesis has occurred.

In the following experiments, one variable in turn was omitted, to demonstrate its necessity in photosynthesis. In each case a **control experiment** was performed in which all variables were present. All leaves used were destarched before the experiment, by keeping the plant in the dark for 48 hours.

Experiment *To investigate the necessity for light in photosynthesis.*

Apparatus

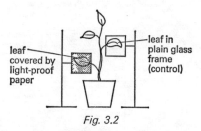

Fig. 3.2

Method A plant was destarched for 48 hours and set up as shown in Fig. 3.2. The plant was left in the Sun for 6 hours, and two leaves detached and tested for starch as described above.

Result Control leaf – blue-black colour with iodine. Paper-covered leaf – no blue-black colour.

Conclusion Absence of starch in the experimental leaf indicates that light was necessary for starch production.

Experiment *To investigate the necessity for carbon dioxide in photosynthesis.*

Apparatus

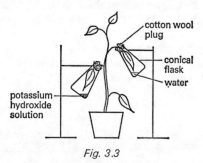

Fig. 3.3

Method One leaf of a destarched plant was enclosed in a conical flask containing a little potassium hydroxide solution (*see* Fig. 3.3). This absorbs carbon dioxide and provides a carbon dioxide-free atmosphere in the flask. Another leaf was similarly enclosed in a flask containing water. This was the control. The plant was left in sunlight for 6 hours and the leaves were then detached and tested for starch.

Result Control leaf – blue-black colour with iodine; CO_2 free leaf – no blue-black colour.

Conclusion The presence of starch in the control leaf, and the absence of starch in the experimental leaf indicated the necessity for carbon dioxide.

The role of carbon dioxide in photosynthesis can be demonstrated by supplying a plant with carbon dioxide containing carbon 14 (a radioactive isotope of carbon). The radioactive carbon appears in a number of organic compounds including carbohydrates, fats and proteins.

Experiment *To investigate the necessity for chlorophyll in photosynthesis.*

Apparatus

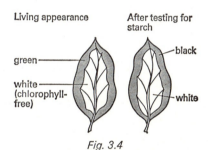

Fig. 3.4

Method A sketch was made of the chlorophyll-free areas on a variegated leaf which had been destarched (*see* Fig. 3.4). It was left on the plant and exposed to sunlight for several hours. It was then tested for starch and the result compared with the original sketch.

Result The original green areas gave a blue-black colouration with iodine. The white areas did not stain blue-black.

Conclusion Starch was only present in the original green areas of the leaf. Therefore photosynthesis only occurs in the presence of chlorophyll.

The following question is typical of many dealing with this topic. You must be certain that you understand how to demonstrate the conditions for photosynthesis and don't forget to include a *control*.

How would you demonstrate that carbon dioxide is necessary for photosynthesis to occur? [8]   (JMB)

Rate of photosynthesis

This depends upon many factors:

1 the amount of light falling on the plant;
2 the leaf surface area and amount of chlorophyll exposed;
3 the number of stomata allowing carbon dioxide into the leaf, and whether they are open or closed (they are generally open in daylight and closed in darkness);
4 the temperature which affects the rate of the dark reaction. The optimum temperature is about 30 °C;
5 the amount of carbon dioxide in the atmosphere (usually 0.04%).

Any one of these factors may limit the rate at which a plant can photosynthesise, provided all other factors are in excess. In a temperate climate, light is often the **limiting factor**. The rate of photosynthesis can be increased by increasing the light available. In a sunny climate, carbon dioxide availability may limit the rate. If the rate of photosynthesis is determined under a series of different light intensities and the results plotted, the graph in Fig. 3.5 shows that the rate rises sharply

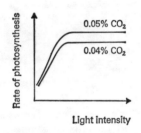

Fig. 3.5 Rate of photosynthesis

and then flattens out at a maximum rate. An increase in light intensity does not increase the rate further. Some other factor, probably carbon dioxide or temperature, is acting as a limiting factor at this level of light intensity. Repeating the experiment under different conditions (e.g. increased carbon dioxide) can affect the rate of photosynthesis as shown on the graph.

Name three external factors which affect the rate of photosynthesis. [3]
(JMB)

Synthesis of other plant materials

Plants manufacture fats, vitamins and proteins from the carbohydrates formed in photosynthesis. The necessary additional elements are obtained from **mineral salts** in the soil. These salts enter the root hairs in solution in (but independently of) the water which passes into the root, and travel through the xylem to the leaf, where the synthesis of these complex substances occurs. The main elements required are:

nitrogen	– for formation of amino acids and subsequently proteins
sulphur	– for healthy root growth
magnesium	– a constituent of chlorophyll
phosphorus	– a constituent of DNA, ATP and some proteins
potassium	– activates enzymes in respiration and photosynthesis
iron	– for chlorophyll formation
calcium	– for formation of cell walls

In addition, minute traces of other elements called **trace elements** are necessary for normal growth, e.g. copper, zinc and manganese.

The effect of a deficiency of a particular element on growth can be shown by '**water culture**' experiments. Similar barley seedlings are grown in a series of solutions. One element is missing from each solution but in all other respects the solution offers the complete mineral needs of the plant. In addition, one plant is grown in a complete solution – the *control*. The solutions and containers are sterilized to prevent fungal growth, and blacked out to exclude algal growth. After a few weeks the seedlings are examined to determine the effect of deficiency of individual elements. The following results may be observed.

> The seedling in the complete culture solution is sturdy, tall and dark green. All the other seedlings are smaller, and in particular those lacking magnesium and iron are yellow. Root formation is retarded in those seedlings lacking sulphur, phosphorus and calcium. Very little growth occurs in plants lacking nitrogen, phosphorus or calcium.

Holozoic nutrition

All animals feed on ready made organic food as they are unable to synthesize organic materials from simple inorganic molecules.

Those living mainly on animal products are called **carnivores**; those feeding on plant food, **herbivores**; those with a mixed diet, **omnivores** (*see* p49).

46 Biology

The characteristics of holozoic nutrition are:

1 ingestion — the intake of complex organic food by animals;
2 digestion — the breakdown of this into small simple soluble molecules;
3 absorption — the uptake of these into living cells;
4 assimilation — the utilization of these to provide energy and the production of new protoplasm;
5 egestion — the removal of undigested waste food materials.

Digestion occurs by mechanical and/or chemical breakdown. The chemical process involved is hydrolysis and enzymes increase the rate of this reaction, e.g.

$$\text{starch} + \text{water} \xrightarrow[\text{(enzyme)}]{\text{amylase}} \text{maltose}$$

Digestion may be **extracellular** (enzymes released onto food in the gut or outside the organism) or **intracellular** (enzymes released within the cells). Study Fig. 3.6 below.

Mechanisms of nutrition

There is a variety of methods of ingestion and you should be familiar with them.

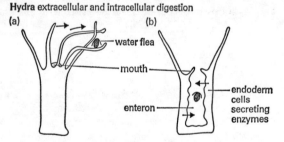

Fig. 3.6 Feeding in *Hydra*

Herring (filter feeder) The stream of water constantly entering the mouth and passing out over the gills, is filtered by the gill rakers, and small organisms are passed back to the oesophagus in a steady stream, to be digested and absorbed (Fig. 3.7).

Locust (chewing mouthparts) An insect has jointed mouthparts which are specialized to deal with a particular type of food (Fig. 3.8). Locusts eat vegetation which is often tough, and they need strong mandibles (jaws).

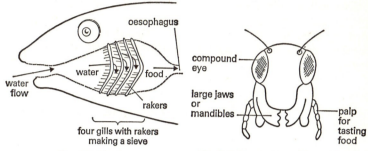

Fig. 3.7 Herring   Fig. 3.8 Front view of locust head

Musca (sucking mouthparts)   The housefly feeds only on liquid food produced by dissolving solid food with saliva (Fig. 3.9).

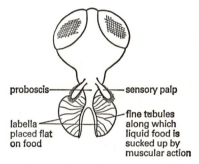

Fig. 3.9 Front of head of housefly

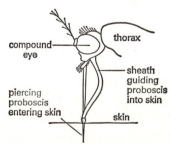

Fig. 3.10 Side view of head of female mosquito feeding

Culex (piercing and sucking mouthparts) The mosquito must first pierce the skin before sucking blood (Fig. 3.10).

Mammalian nutrition

Mammals ingest food through the mouth, where the teeth play a large part in preparation of the food for digestion. **Mastication** is the mechanical breakdown of food by the teeth, aided by the tongue and jaw muscles.

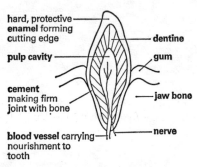

Fig. 3.11 V.S. incisor tooth of mammal

It is always worth learning Fig. 3.11. It is simple and is a fairly common question in examinations.

(a) *Make a labelled diagram to show the structure of a mammalian tooth.* [8]
(b) *In what ways do teeth of mammals differ from those of other vertebrates?* [2] (o)

The teeth of all other vertebrates are all alike – just simple pegs (**homodont** teeth). The teeth of mammals are varied in shape and arrangement according to function and diet (**heterodont** teeth).

Incisors Present at front of mouth for biting or gnawing.
Canines 'Eye' teeth developed as fangs in carnivores.
Premolars⎫ Cheek teeth with double roots, used for chewing,
Molars   ⎭ grinding or crushing.

All mammalian teeth except molars are represented in the **milk dentition** present in the young animal. The milk teeth are pushed out as the permanent teeth develop.

1 **Herbivorous dentition** (e.g. sheep) Lower incisors grip against

horny pad on upper jaw, to tear grass. Have **diastema** – space on jaw between incisors and cheek teeth. No canines. Cheek teeth ridged for chewing. Jaw action across ridges for maximum grinding of cellulose walls of plant food. Premolars and molars similar.

2 **Carnivorous dentition** (e.g. dog) Incisors pointed. Canines well developed for seizing and killing prey. Cheek teeth with pointed cusps for crushing. Fourth premolar in upper jaw, and first molar in lower jaw especially large and modified for shearing flesh and bone (**carnassial teeth**).

3 **Omnivorous dentition** (e.g. man) Incisors flat for biting all types of food. Canines present but not large. Cheek teeth have rounded cusps for chewing a mixed diet.

Nutrition in man

The following classes of food are essential to maintain health in man: carbohydrates, fats, proteins, vitamins, mineral salts, water and roughage.

Diet in man

A *balanced diet* supplies the necessary classes of food in adequate amounts and correct proportions to maintain healthy active life and if necessary, growth. It must supply not only the necessary chemical constituents, but also sufficient energy for the needs of the body (*see* p64). The main energy-producing foods are carbohydrate and fat.

Average daily energy requirements vary according to:

sex – adult man = 12 000 kJ; adult woman = 9600 kJ
activity – physically demanding job, e.g. coal-miner = 50 000 kJ
age – children require more in proportion to body size = 9000 kJ

The amount of energy-giving foods in the diet should match these requirements. The type of food required varies too:

children and pregnant women – extra protein and vitamins;

nursing mothers – extra fluid and protein, usually supplied by milk;
babies – milk, an almost perfect food, lacks iron, but usually sufficient stored in baby's body from birth;
elderly people and those in sedentary occupations – more fresh fruit and vegetables for vitamins and roughage, and less carbohydrate and fat.

Table 3.1 Food requirements of man

Food	Function	Sources
Carbohydrates	Release of energy	
Starch		Flour products, potato, cane sugar
Complex sugars – sucrose maltose		
Simple sugars – glucose		Honey, fruit
Proteins	Growth and repair of tissues	
1st class		Meat, milk, eggs, cheese, peas, beans
2nd class (as amino acids)		
Fats (as fatty acids and glycerol)	Storage; release of energy	Milk, cream, cheese, butter, plant oils
Vitamins		
A	Health of mucous membranes; resistance to infection; vision in dim light	Butter, milk, carrots, vegetables
B	Health of nervous system; release of energy	Wheatgerm, liver, yeast
C	Health of skin and blood vessels	Fresh citrus fruits
D	Bone development	Fish liver oil, butter
Salts		
sodium	⎰ Constituents of	
potassium	⎱ blood and cells	
calcium	Bones and teeth formation	Milk, fruit and vegetables
iron	Haemoglobin formation	
iodine	Thyroid gland function	
phosphorus	Bones, teeth, ATP, DNA	
Water	Constituent of cells and body fluids; solvent for chemicals taking part in all living processes	
Roughage	No food value; stimulates muscle in wall of alimentary canal	Fruit and vegetable fibres

Table 3.2 Chemical tests for food substances

Food	Test	Result
Starch	Add 1–2 drops dilute brown **iodine/ potassium iodide solution** to a starch suspension.	Intense blue-black colouration
Reducing sugar (glucose, maltose)	Add an equal quantity of blue **Benedict's reagent** to a glucose solution and boil.	Brick-red precipitate
Protein	Add **Millon's reagent** and warm.	White cloudy precipitate turning red on warming
Fat	1 Rub into filter paper.	Makes a grease spot
	2 Add osmic acid.	Stains black
	3 Dissolve in ethanol. Pour solution into water.	Milky emulsion

Alimentary canal

The digestive system of man is a muscular tube running from mouth to anus, and specialized to perform different functions in different regions.

Table 3.3 Functions of different parts of human digestive system

Specialized part	Function
buccal cavity	ingestion, mastication
pharynx	swallowing
oesophagus	links pharynx to stomach
stomach	food storage and digestion of protein
duodenum	digestion and absorption
liver (bile)	emulsification of fats
pancreas (pancreatic juice)	digestion of fat, protein, starch
ileum	completion of digestion and absorption of food
colon	absorption of water
rectum	formation and storage of faeces
anus	egestion

Buccal cavity Following ingestion, the food is broken down into small pieces by the teeth exposing a large surface area for the action of digestive enzymes. It is mixed with saliva from three pairs of salivary glands. This

1 moistens food for swallowing,
2 dissolves soluble food,
3 digests cooked starch by the action of salivary amylase, to form maltose.

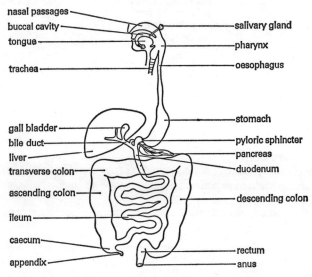

Fig. 3.12 The alimentary canal in man

Experiment *To investigate the action of salivary amylase.*

Method A specimen of freshly collected saliva was divided into two equal parts and one part was thoroughly boiled. Boiling denatures protein and destroys the enzyme amylase. The unboiled saliva was added to a sample of 1% starch solution labelled A, and the boiled saliva to a similar sample labelled C. This was the control experiment in which conditions are similar except for the absence of the active enzyme. Both tubes were left for 10 minutes in a water bath at 37 °C. A few drops of solution were removed from tube A and added to 1–2 drops of dilute iodine/potassium iodide solution. The result was recorded. To the rest of the solution in A, an equal quantity of Benedict's solution was added and boiled. The result was recorded. These tests were repeated for tube C.

Results Tube A With iodine: brown colour of iodine remained.
  With Benedict's: brick-red precipitate formed.
 Tube C With iodine: blue-black colouration formed.
  With Benedict's: original blue colour remained.

Conclusion There is no starch present in A at the end of the experiment. Reducing sugar is present in A. Starch is present in C, but there is no reducing sugar. In tube A starch has been changed to reducing sugar. In tube C the starch is unchanged. Since all other conditions in the two tubes were identical, the differences in the two tubes must result from the presence of active amylase in A.

In order to investigate the effect of temperature on enzyme activity, repeat this experiment using the same amounts of starch and enzyme for a range of temperatures from 5 °C–65 °C at 10 °C intervals. Ensure that starch and enzyme solutions and test-tubes are at the appropriate temperature before mixing. Record the time taken for blue-black colour of starch to disappear and plot a graph of time against temperature and make your conclusions about the effect of temperature on enzyme action.

Using the information given above answer the question below. Great emphasis should be placed on giving all practical details, e.g. accurate temperatures, stated volumes and colours involved in the food test.

Describe with full practical details, an experiment you would perform to show the effect of temperature on enzyme action. [14] (O)

For further details of enzyme activity *see* p34.
  Here is another problem for you to solve:

Two solutions, neither of which contained a reducing sugar were mixed and left overnight at room temperature. On testing the resulting liquid for reducing sugars the following morning, a positive result was obtained. Suggest the nature of the two original solutions. [2] (JMB)

Swallowing The food is formed into an oval mass called a **bolus** by the action of the tongue, and pushed backwards against the roof of the mouth. This starts a reflex action which results in the bolus being pushed into the **oesophagus** by the contraction of the walls of the **pharynx**. To prevent food from entering the respiratory passages, the **soft palate** closes the opening into the nasal passages and the **epiglottis** closes the **larynx**.

The walls of the oesophagus convey the bolus to the stomach by **peristalsis**. This is a wave-like muscular action involving the longitudinal and circular muscles of the oesophagus.

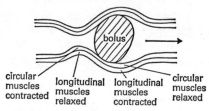

Fig. 3.13 Peristalsis in the oesophagus

Stomach This is a J-shaped organ with muscular walls and a glandular lining. **Gastric glands** open into the stomach and discharge gastric juice which contains:

1 **hydrochloric acid** – stops salivary amylase action and provides the correct pH for pepsin action;
2 **pepsin** – hydrolyses protein to polypeptides;
3 **rennin** – is only valuable in young mammals living entirely on milk. It clots milk, retaining it in the stomach for pepsin action.

The stomach has the following functions:

1 digestion of protein;
2 formation of a creamy **chyme** by the churning action of stomach muscles;
3 temporary storage of food which is passed on to the duodenum in small portions for further digestion.

The lower opening of the stomach can be closed by a ring of muscle called the **pyloric sphincter**. After a meal, it opens at intervals to allow small amounts of chyme through to the duodenum. This control prevents a large mass of acidic stomach contents from entering the duodenum.

Duodenum The first 12 inches of the small intestine. Secretions from three glands mix with food here. They are all alkaline and provide the correct pH for the digestive enzymes.

1 **Bile** – greenish-yellow colour, produced by the liver, concentrated in the **gall bladder**, passed to duodenum by **bile duct** when food present. It contains sodium bicarbonate which neutralizes stomach acid, and bile salts which emulsify fats and activate the enzyme, lipase.
2 **Pancreatic juice** – produced by **pancreas**, enters duodenum by the **pancreatic duct**, contains three enzymes which have the following effects:

 (a) starch + water $\xrightarrow{\text{amylase}}$ maltose

 (b) fat + water $\xrightarrow{\text{lipase}}$ fatty acids + glycerol

 (c) **trypsinogen + enterokinase** $\longrightarrow$ **trypsin**
  $\downarrow$
  proteins + water $\longrightarrow$ peptides and amino acids

3 **Succus entericus** – produced by glands in the wall of the duodenum, contains several enzymes which complete digestion.

 (a) peptides + water $\xrightarrow{\text{erespin}}$ amino acids

 (b) trypsinogen $\xrightarrow{\text{enterokinase}}$ trypsin
  (inactive enzyme)   (active enzyme)

 (c) sucrose + water $\xrightarrow{\text{invertase}}$ glucose + fructose

 (d) maltose + water $\xrightarrow{\text{maltase}}$ glucose

 (e) lactose + water $\xrightarrow{\text{lactase}}$ glucose + galactose

All digestible food is now soluble and of small molecular size, and can be absorbed.

Ileum The longest part of the small intestine, and the site of absorption of digested food into the circulatory system. The efficiency of uptake is increased by **villi** – finger-like projections from the already folded lining of the ileum. These give an enormous surface area for absorption.

Other features of the villi which increase the rate of absorption are shown in Fig. 3.14.

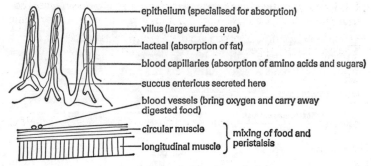

Fig. 3.14 Part of the ileum wall

The digested food is distributed round the body in the blood stream and absorption is only complete when it has entered the cells of the body (*see* p92) where assimilation occurs.

Name any four substances which are absorbed from the digested food in the small intestine. [4] (O & C)

Caecum and appendix Reduced in size in man and have no special function (*see* herbivores p49).

Colon Main function is the absorption of water from the fluid contents. This leaves a semi-solid mass of faeces which is moved into the rectum by 'mass peristalsis' before **defaecation**.

Rectum After further water absorption, the contents of the rectum consisting largely of undigested cellulose and other plant fibres, bacteria and dead cells form the faeces. These are eliminated at intervals through the anus by the process of **egestion**.

Variation in the alimentary canal of herbivores

The basic structure and function is the same as in man but you should note the following differences:

1 The intestine is usually longer in proportion to the size of the animal because plant food takes longer to digest.
2 The stomach of non-ruminants, e.g. horse, is small. They eat almost continuously because of the relatively low nutritional value of plant food.

3 The stomach of **ruminants,** e.g. cow, has several chambers. A large quantity of food is ingested in a short time, and passes into the rumen. It is later regurgitated and thoroughly chewed before passing into the true stomach. This adaptation minimizes the time spent by some ruminants, e.g. deer, feeding in possible danger in the open.
4 The caecum and appendix in, e.g. the rabbit, are very large. Here bacteria digest cellulose, an important constituent of plant food which is not available to vertebrates because they do not possess the enzyme necessary to hydrolyse it.

$$\text{cellulose} \xrightarrow{\text{bacterial enzymes}} \text{glucose which can be absorbed by the rabbit}$$

The liver

The liver is the largest organ within the body. It is red-brown in colour and lies in the abdomen immediately below the diaphragm.

Vessels entering the liver:

1 **hepatic artery** bringing oxygenated blood from the aorta;
2 **hepatic portal vein** carrying absorbed food from the alimentary canal (a portal vein is a blood vessel with capillaries at both ends).

Vessels leaving the liver:

1 **hepatic vein** carrying all blood from liver to vena cava;
2 **bile duct** carrying bile from liver to the duodenum. The **gall bladder** lies on this duct.

The liver is an important *homeostatic* organ. All absorbed food substances pass through the liver before reaching the tissues. This enables their levels to be regulated according to the needs of the body. Most of these regulatory processes are described elsewhere in the book. Check the details of each of these on the appropriate page as you read through the revision summary.

Functions of the liver
1 Control of constant blood sugar level. Excess sugar in the diet is converted to glycogen (insoluble) under the influence of insulin. When sugar is required to supply energy it can be converted back to glucose (p58).
2 Removal of lactic acid from the blood and its conversion to glycogen.
3 Conversion of fat to glycogen. This process is reversible depending on diet and energy needs of the body.

4 Formation of plasma proteins – albumen, globulin, fibrinogen and prothrombin.
5 Formation of urea from excess amino acids which cannot be stored.
6 Storage of vitamins A; B_{12}; D (p50).
7 Storage of iron – old red blood cells are removed from circulation and their haemoglobin is broken down. Iron is stored and the rest excreted as bile pigments.
8 Formation of bile (p55).
9 Detoxication of poisons.
10 Production of body heat – main source of this because of liver's size and activity.

Notice that most of these functions involve food substances, and the first seven are arranged according to their association with carbohydrates, fats, proteins, vitamins, mineral salts.

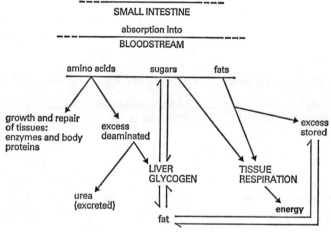

Fig. 3.15 Utilization of food: summary

Saprophytic nutrition

Plants without chlorophyll cannot photosynthesize and must obtain organic food already synthesized. Some organisms, e.g. moulds, yeasts and bacteria, feed saprophytically, i.e. on non-living organic matter. They play an important part in the breakdown of dead animal and plant material (*see* p203).

Mucor is a mould living on bread, jam, damp leather and other moist organic matter (Fig. 3.16). The tips of the **hyphae** secrete hydrolysing enzymes onto the food (extra-cellular digestion). The soluble food is absorbed by the hyphae, and used in growth and energy production.

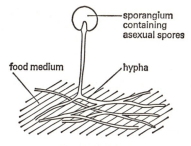

Fig. 3.16 Mucor

Parasitic nutrition

Organisms living at the expense of a living host may be **endoparasites** – living inside the body of the host, or **ectoparasites** – living on the surface of the host's body (*see* p217).

Parasites are very specific and specialized and show many modifications associated with their host and its way of life, e.g. the tapeworm in man has

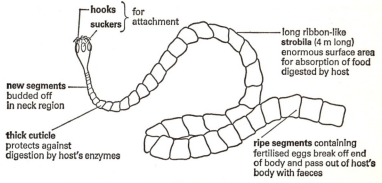

Fig. 3.17 Tapeworm

1 hooks and suckers for attachment;
2 reduction in locomotory organs especially muscle;
3 reduction in sense organs;

4 reduction in alimentary canal since food already soluble;
5 no mouth, but large surface area for food absorption;
6 protective cuticle and anti-enzymes secreted to prevent digestion by host;
7 hermaphrodite with large numbers of gametes to ensure fertilization;
8 shelled embryo for protection;
9 complex life-cycle with intermediate host, the pig, to ensure transfer to new host.

The information given in this section should enable you to answer the following question.

Distinguish carefully between saprophytic and parasitic modes of feeding.
[4] (LOND)

Key words

autotrophic
heterotrophic
holozoic
ingestion
digestion
absorption
assimilation
egestion
saprophytic
parastitic
host
carbohydrates
photosynthesis
fats
mineral salts
vitamins
amino acids
carbon dioxide
stomata
chloroplasts
water
xylem
light

light reaction
dark reaction
sugars
phloem
limiting factor
mineral salts
trace elements
water culture
carnivores
herbivores
omnivores
extracellular digestion
intracellular digestion
mastication
homodont
heterodont
incisor
canines
premolars
molars
milk dentition
diastema
carnassial teeth

roughage
iodine/potassium iodide
Benedict's reagent
Millon's reagent
balanced diet
alimentary canal
buccal cavity
pharynx
oesophagus
stomach
duodenum
liver
bile
pancreas
pancreatic juice
ileum
colon
rectum
anus
enzymes
salivary amylase
bolus

tongue	lipase	defaecation
soft palate	trypsinogen	egestion
epiglottis	enterokinase	ruminants
larynx	trypsin	hepatic artery
peristalsis	succus entericus	hepatic portal vein
gastric glands	erepsin	hepatic vein
hydrochloric acid	sucrase	bile duct
pepsin	maltase	gall bladder
rennin	lactase	hyphae
chyme	villi	endoparasite
pyloric sphincter	caecum	ectoparasite
emulsify	appendix	

Past examinations questions

1 *To complete the statement below on plant nutrition use each of the following words once only:*
carbon dioxide; cortex; carbohydrate; oxygen; phloem; photosynthesis; root hairs; starch; xylem. [9]

In the nutrition of a green plant water enters the . . . passes across the . . . of the root, and enters a . . . vessel which forms a continuous tube to the leaf. Here . . . takes place and the water is split into hydrogen and . . . The gas, . . . which has entered the leaf by the stomata is now reduced to a soluble . . . which returns to the root via the . . . where it is converted into . . . an insoluble storage material. (O sentence completion)

2 *When a leaf is tested for starch, it is first placed in boiling water. It is transferred to alcohol and heated in a water bath. Next it is rinsed in water. Finally it is soaked in iodine in potassium iodide solution.*
 (a) *Suggest one reason for first boiling the leaf.*
 (b) *Why should the alcohol be heated in a water bath and not heated directly over a flame?*
 (c) *Describe two changes produced in the leaf by the hot alcohol.*
 (d) *State one reason for rinsing the leaf in water.*
 (e) *Describe the result if the starch test is negative.* (AEB short answer)

3 *Describe four important processes concerned with digestion that take place in the buccal cavity.* (CAM)

4 *In photosynthesis, solar energy (sunlight) is converted into chemical energy within a carbohydrate molecule.*

(i) Write an equation, in words or symbols, to show the beginning and end products of photosynthesis.
(ii) What part does light play in the intermediate stages of photosynthesis? (AEB)

5 What are the conditions necessary for the formation of carbohydrate in a leaf? [4]
How would you demonstrate experimentally that two of the conditions you have mentioned are necessary? [16]   (O & C)

6 All growing cells need a supply of amino acids with which to make the proteins of protoplasm. (a) Name a food from which man obtains essential amino acids. (b) Name three raw materials needed by plants to make amino acids.   (AEB)

7 Each of the statements (a) to (d) describe a process that occurs in animal nutrition. Name each process.
(a) Enzymes, made in the cytoplasm, pass out of a cell on to food.
(b) Maltose is converted to glucose.
(c) Amino acids pass from food into the cytoplasm.
(d) Undigested material passes out of the body.   (AEB)

8 In the liver, what happens to an excess of the following food requirements? (a) amino acids, (b) vitamin D? [2]   (SCE)

9 (a) For each of the following food materials describe **one** test you would use to show its presence:
(i) a reducing sugar, (ii) starch, (iii) a protein, (iv) a fat. [15]
(b) In the digestion of each of the following food materials: starch; protein; fat; name **one** enzyme that is used. In each case, what end products are formed? [3, 3]   (O)

10 Which one of the following would be an example of saprophytism?
A A fungus living on manure
B A locust feeding on a maize crop
C A hermit crab living inside the shell of a whelk
D Ivy growing on an oak tree
E A roundworm feeding in the bloodstream of a horse. [1]   (JMB)

4 Respiration

Respiration The liberation of energy by the breakdown of food molecules.
Energy The capacity to do work.
Fermentation The process of anaerobic respiration in yeasts and some bacteria.
Ventilation The production of an increased flow of air or water over the gas exchange surface.
Inspiration The passage of air or water containing oxygen into an organism by muscular movement.
Expiration The passage of air or water containing carbon dioxide out of an organism by muscular movement.
Diffusion The movement of molecules down a concentration gradient from a region of their high concentration to a region of their low concentration.
Metabolic rate The rate at which respiration occurs in living organisms.
Compensation point The point at which the rates of photosynthesis and respiration are equal.

Energy

Energy cannot be created or destroyed. It may occur in many forms, e.g. heat, light, sound, electrical, chemical and mechanical, and these can be changed from one form into another (i.e. they are interconvertible).

$$\text{light (sun)} \xrightarrow{\text{photosynthesis}} \text{chemical (sugars in plant)} \xrightarrow{\text{feeding, digestion and respiration}} \text{mechanical (muscle contraction in animals)}$$

All living cells require a continual supply of energy in order to carry out a variety of processes vital to life. These include:

1 mechanical contraction of muscle (movement);
2 chemical synthesis of substances;
3 growth and division of cells;
4 active transport of substances into and out of cells;
5 electrical transmission of nerve impulses;
6 maintenance of a constant body temperature (birds and mammals).

The above are forms of work carried out by living organisms.

All the energy used by living organisms comes from the Sun in the form of light waves. The only organisms capable of trapping the light energy supply are the plants which carry out photosynthesis. Light energy from the Sun cannot be stored so plants convert this into chemical energy, as shown above.

The light energy is used to convert carbon dioxide and water into glucose. The energy is stored in the chemical bonds holding the atoms together in these molecules (see p66).

$$\text{carbon dioxide} + \text{water} \xrightarrow[\text{(chlorophyll)}]{\text{light energy (sunlight)}} \text{glucose} + \text{oxygen} \\ \text{(food)}$$

$$6CO_2 + 6H_2O \longrightarrow C_6H_{12}O_6 + 6O_2 \\ \text{(chemical energy)}$$

Plants are able to store this manufactured food as starch or sugars. Plants provide energy for all other forms of life. They are the 'primary producers' that form the basis of all food chains (see p209).

This energy cannot be used by plants or animals for any of the processes vital to life until it is released from the food molecules in which it is stored. This process, by which energy is released from food substances is called **respiration**.

Respiration

Respiration is a characteristic feature of all living organisms. There are two forms of respiration called aerobic respiration and anaerobic respiration.

Aerobic respiration

This occurs in most organisms and depends upon a constant supply of oxygen. It is basically a chemical reaction which may be represented as follows:

$$\text{carbohydrate} + \text{oxygen} \xrightarrow{\text{enzymes}} \text{carbon dioxide} + \text{water} + \text{energy}$$

used ↓ for **work**

The energy released comes from the breakdown of glucose molecules in the presence of oxygen and the process is called cell respiration.

Cell respiration (tissue or internal respiration)

Raw materials enter the cell, respiration occurs and waste products are removed (*see* Fig. 4.1). Inside the cell, enzymes break down the glucose

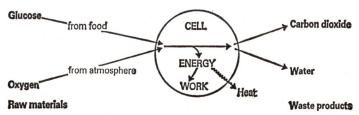

Fig. 4.1 Summary of cell respiration

molecule in a series of stages. Each stage is controlled by a different enzyme and a small amount of the total energy of the molecule is released.

```
glucose
   \
   enzyme 1
      \
       B + energy
        \
        enzyme 2
           \
            C + energy
           several stages
              \
               carbon dioxide + water
```

The overall reaction may be represented as

$$C_6H_{12}O_6 + 6O_2 \xrightarrow{enzymes} 6CO_2 + 6H_2O + 2880 \text{ kJ}$$
glucose   oxygen   carbon   water   energy
                                dioxide

In the many **mitochondria** of each cell this energy is used to manufacture molecules of an energy rich compound called **adenosine triphosphate** (ATP) as follows:

adenosine diphosphate (ADP) + phosphate
$$\xrightarrow{\text{energy (from breakdown of glucose)}} \text{adenosine triphosphate (ATP)}$$

$$\text{A-P-P} + \text{P} \xrightarrow{\text{energy}} \text{A-P-P}\sim\text{P}$$

ATP is the intermediate energy compound in the cell. If the energy in the glucose molecules were released suddenly the cell would be destroyed by the excess heat. When released slowly some of the energy can be harnessed for work by the cell.

The chemical bond $\sim$P is 'energy-rich' and when broken down provides energy for cell work.

$$\text{ATP} \xrightarrow{\text{enzyme}} \text{ADP} + \text{P} + \textbf{energy}$$
$$\downarrow$$
$$\text{work}$$

This is a quick, simple reaction and energy can, in this way, be provided instantly when needed.

(a) *Name the structures inside a cell in which adenosine triphosphate (ATP) is produced.*
(b) *How are the substances ATP and adenosine diphosphate (ADP) involved in the storage and use of energy within a cell?* (AEB)

The amount of energy released by an organism in a given time is known as the **metabolic rate**. Wherever energy is transferred from one compound to another or used in work some is lost as heat energy. This is usually considered as lost or wasted energy but homoiothermic animals (birds and mammals) can control their heat loss and use it in order to maintain a constant body temperature (*see* p113).

The removal of the waste products of respiration from the cell is called excretion (*see* p103).

Experiment *To investigate heat production during respiration in seeds.*

Apparatus

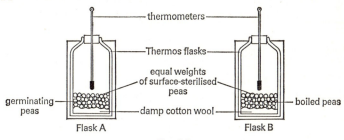

Fig. 4.2

Method Germinating peas require energy released by respiration. Some energy is released as heat and a rise in temperature in the apparatus is used to indicate respiration is occurring. The apparatus was set up as shown in Fig. 4.2. Surface sterilization in sodium hypochlorite solution prevents bacterial and fungal growth. Boiling the peas in flask **B** destroyed all enzymes involved in respiration. This acts as a control.

Table 4.1 Results

Day	Temperature (°C) Flask A	Flask B
1	21	20
2	22	19
3	25	20
4	25	20

Conclusion No heat was released in flask B as no respiration occurred. The fluctuation in temperature in flask B probably resulted from a fluctuation in room temperature. The rise in temperature in flask A resulted from heat produced by germinating peas during respiration.

Details from the above experiment and the one on p68 may be used in answering the question given on p84.

Anaerobic respiration
The breakdown of glucose in the absence of oxygen occurs in some fungi, bacteria and skeletal muscle during vigorous exercise. It is not as

efficient as aerobic respiration in terms of energy production and ATP yield. The waste products vary as shown below and may be economically important.

Anaerobic respiration in yeast (fermentation)
This process is important in the baking and brewing industries. Single celled yeasts grow and divide very rapidly and obtain their energy by breaking down sugars as shown below:

$$C_6H_{12}O_6 \longrightarrow 2C_2H_5OH + 2CO_2 + 210 \text{ kJ}$$
glucose   ethyl alcohol   carbon   energy
                            dioxide

The waste products are ethyl alcohol and carbon dioxide. Carbon dioxide is used to make dough rise and the alcohol produced by brewer's yeast is used in beer and wine making.

Experiment *To investigate carbon dioxide production by yeast during anaerobic respiration.*

Apparatus

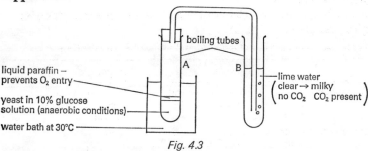

Fig. 4.3

Method A yeast and glucose solution was made up using boiled water (contains no air), set up as shown in Fig. 4.3 and left for 2 hours.

Results The lime water turns milky as gas produced in Tube A bubbles through it.

Conclusion The gas produced by the yeast cells during the anaerobic breakdown of glucose contains carbon dioxide.

Anaerobic respiration in skeletal muscle
During vigorous activity oxygen supply to the cells becomes insufficient despite faster breathing. Anaerobic respiration occurs at the same time

as aerobic and supplies extra energy for muscle contraction. **Lactic acid** accumulates and an **oxygen debt** is incurred.

glucose ⟶ lactic acid + energy

The lactic acid enters the blood stream and passes to the liver where it is converted to glucose as the oxygen debt is repaid. The glucose is returned to the muscle and stored as glycogen.

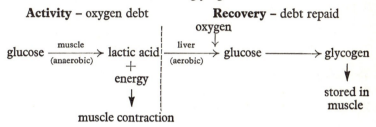

The above information is required in answering the following question:

Give the name of the substance which accumulates in the muscles of man during vigorous exercise. [1]
Why must the rate of breathing remain high for some time after the period of exercise is over? [1]   (SCE)

Table 4.2 Comparison of aerobic and anaerobic respiration

	Aerobic	Anaerobic
Occurrence	Most animal and plant cells	Some fungi and bacteria; skeletal muscle
Energy released per glucose molecule	High (2800 kJ)	Low (210 kJ)
ATP production	High	Low
End products	Carbon dioxide, water	Ethyl alcohol and carbon dioxide, or lactic acid

Give three differences between aerobic and anaerobic respiration. [3]   (O)

Gas exchange (external respiration)

All aerobic organisms require oxygen for respiration and produce carbon dioxide as a waste product. There is a continual exchange of these gases between the atmosphere and the cell.

The movement of these gases occurs by **diffusion** (*see* p63). This is the movement of molecules down a concentration gradient from a region of *their* high concentration to a region of *their* low concentration.

Diffusion gradients are always maintained between atmosphere and cell because cells use up oxygen and produce carbon dioxide.

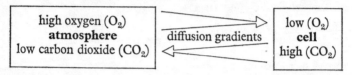

Gas exchange occurs through a **gas exchange surface**. In all cells this is the **cell membrane**.

In small simple organisms, e.g. *Amoeba*, *Hydra*, gas exchange occurs over the whole outer surface of the organism. As organisms increase in size and complexity two problems arise:

1 the ratio of their surface area:volume decreases and direct diffusion becomes inadequate;
2 the distance between the environment and the cell increases.

Direct diffusion between environment and cell is insufficient for gas exchange and a transport system is required. A specialized gas exchange surface becomes necessary at the point where environment and transport system meet, e.g. the gill.

All gas exchange surfaces have the following features which permit diffusion. They are

1 thin,
2 moist,
3 possess large surface area,
4 permeable to gases.

As animals increase in size their energy demands increase. More oxygen is required and their gas exchange surface must also be

5 well ventilated and
6 have a good blood supply containing a respiratory pigment, e.g. haemoglobin (this is most important in birds and mammals since they have a high metabolic rate).

You should learn these features. They are vital to all answers dealing with gas exchange and may themselves form part of a question, e.g.

Respiration

Name three characteristics possessed by surfaces involved in respiratory exchange. (AEB)

There are five types of gas exchange surface and each is suited to work in a particular environment.

1 cell membrane } aquatic
2 gills
3 epidermis (skin) semi-aquatic
4 tracheoles } terrestrial
5 lungs

You should be familiar with gas exchange mechanisms in a variety of organisms. In each case remember that the basic principles are common to all. Past questions are given for you to answer as part of your revision.

Gas exchange in Protozoa – e.g. *Amoeba*

The method of gas exchange is very similar to that in cells of all multicellular plants and animals. The gas exchange surface is the cell membrane. It is thin, moist (surrounded by water), has a large surface area to volume ratio and is permeable to respiratory gases. Exchange of gases occurs across the whole of the cell membrane as shown below.

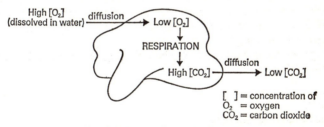

Fig. 4.4 Gas exchange in *Amoeba*

Gas exchange in insects, e.g. locust

Most insects are terrestrial and face a problem of water loss. To prevent them becoming dehydrated they are covered by a waterproof cuticle. This acts as a barrier to gas exchange. Openings to the atmosphere are found in the cuticle of the thorax and abdomen. These are called **spiracles** and sometimes act as valves allowing gases to pass into and out of fine tubes called **tracheae**. Tracheae run throughout the body and end in the tissues as tiny tubes called **tracheoles**. These are kept moist and are the site of gas exchange. The whole system is called the

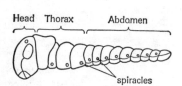

Fig. 4.5 Position of spiracles in the locust

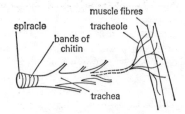

Fig. 4.6 Tracheal system

tracheal system. The route taken by oxygen and carbon dioxide is shown in the diagram below, where the arrows represent diffusion pathways.

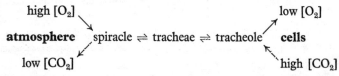

To prevent water loss the spiracles are kept closed as much as possible. Some insects show pumping movements of the abdomen which squeeze air in and out of the tracheal system. This is called **ventilation** and aids diffusion and increases the rate of gas exchange.

Explain briefly three ways in which the tracheal system of an insect is suited to its function of gas exchange. [3]   (JMB)

Gas exchange in fish, e.g. goldfish

Gas exchange occurs by a system of **gills** (*see* Fig. 4.7). On each side of the head are a series of openings called **gill slits** which connect the pharynx to the **opercular cavity**. This area is protected on the outside

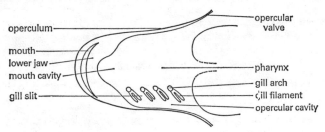

Fig. 4.7 Gill region (detail of one side only)

Respiration 73

by a flap of tissue called the **operculum**. Between each gill slit is a structure called the **gill arch** supported by bone. From each gill arch **gill filaments** project and their surface area is increased by the presence of **gill lamellae**. The walls of the lamellae are only one cell thick and well supplied with blood containing haemoglobin. This is the site of gas exchange. Oxygen dissolved in the water diffuses into the blood and combines with haemoglobin. Carbon dioxide dissolved in the blood passes out into the water (*see* diagram below – arrows indicate diffusion pathways).

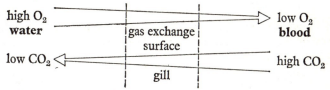

A continuous current of water passing over the gills is produced by volume and pressure changes in the mouth, pharynx and opercular cavities.

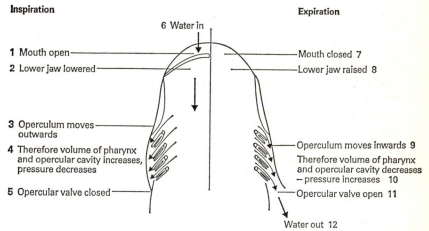

Fig. 4.8 Inspiration and expiration in fish

The volume of a body and the pressure within it are related so that as either increases the other decreases. Therefore

as volume increases ⟶ pressure decreases
as volume decreases ⟶ pressure increases

Muscular movements (ventilation) produce these changes in volume and pressure and ensure a continuous flow of water over the gills. This flow of water can be considered in two stages shown in Fig. 4.8.

Describe the route taken, the organs used and chemical changes involved in the passage of oxygen from the air to the muscles in the body of a fish.
[8] (O & C)

Gas exchange through epidermis (skin)

In the earthworm, gas exchange occurs across the entire outer surface – the skin (**epidermis**). This has all the features of a gas exchange surface and is adequate to supply the small volume of oxygen needed in respiration.

In the frog, gas exchange may occur through the lungs, mouth and skin. When the frog is inactive, enough oxygen can be taken up by the mouth and skin to supply all respiratory needs. The skin alone is used during hibernation.

In both the earthworm and frog concentration gradients are maintained by the rapid passage of blood through the skin. Beneath the thin epidermis is a network of capillaries where gas exchange between environment and blood takes place (*see* Fig. 4.9).

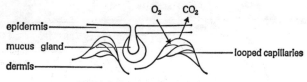

Fig. 4.9 Section through frog skin

Gas exchange in mammals (e.g. man)

Gas exchange in man occurs in the **lungs**. These are suited to exchange of gases in the terrestrial environment. The lungs are situated inside the body to prevent excess water loss.

The two lungs are situated in the air-tight **thoracic cavity**. This is a sealed cavity protected by the **sternum, ribs** and **intercostal muscles** at the front and sides and the vertebral column at the back. The muscular diaphragm separates the thorax from the abdominal cavity.

Air enters the nose and mouth and passes through the **pharynx** and **larynx** (voice-box) to the **trachea** (wind-pipe). Food is prevented from entering the trachea by the **epiglottis** (Fig. 4.10). The trachea is kept open by rings of cartilage and its lining is covered with cilia. Mucus is

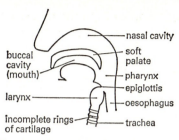

Fig. 4.10 Upper part of respiratory tract

secreted by the nose and the trachea to keep the surface moist, to warm in-coming air and to trap dust and bacteria. Upward beating of the cilia carries the mucus up to the pharynx where it is swallowed as phlegm.

At its base the trachea branches, forming right and left **bronchi**. These branch to form many **bronchioles** which end in structures resembling bunches of grapes called **alveoli**. Each alveolus is covered by capillaries and this is the site of gas exchange (Fig. 4.11).

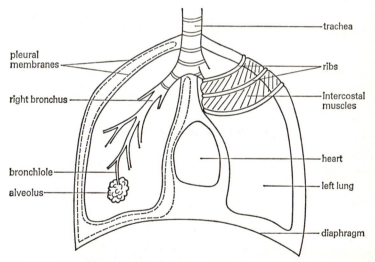

Fig. 4.11 Lungs and associated structures

Pleural membranes cover the lungs and line the thoracic cavity. Between the membranes is the pleural cavity containing pleural fluid to lubricate the lungs during breathing (ventilation) movements.

Breathing (ventilation of the lungs)

Breathing movements are produced by the contraction and relaxation of the diaphragm and intercostal muscles. This alters the volume of the thorax and produces pressure changes. Air is forced into the lungs when the pressure in them falls below that of the atmosphere. This is **inspiration**. When the pressure in the lungs rises above that of the atmosphere air is passed out in **expiration** (Fig. 4.12).

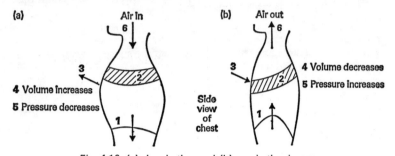

Fig. 4.12 (a) Inspiration and (b) expiration in man

Table 4.3 Process of breathing

		Inspiration	Expiration
1	Diaphragm	Contracts (moves down)	Relaxes (moves up)
2	External intercostal muscles	Contract	Relax
3	Rib cage	Moves up and out	Moves down and in
4	Volume of thorax	Increases	Decreases
5	Pressure of thorax	Decreases	Increases
6	Air moves	Into lungs	Out of lungs

Capacities of lungs – approximate values for adult man

Total capacity   – volume of lungs when fully inflated – 5 litre.

Vital capacity   – volume of air passing in and out of lungs during forced breathing – 4 litre.

Tidal air   – volume of air passing in and out of lungs during normal breathing – 0.5 litre.

Residual air   – volume of air which cannot be removed from lungs by breathing out (mainly in alveoli) – 1 litre.

Questions dealing with the topic of breathing occur quite frequently and you should ensure that it is understood.

(a) *List in order the parts through which tidal air passes.*
(b) *Where is residual air found?*
(c) *Describe the mechanism of inhalation (breathing in).* (AEB)

Gas exchange at the alveoli

There are approximately 700 million alveoli in the lungs. They have the following features,

1 thin – walls only one cell thick
2 moist
3 large surface area
4 permeable to respiratory gases
} which allow diffusion to occur

5 well ventilated
6 good blood supply
} which maintain steep concentration gradients

The exchange of gases is shown in Fig. 4.13.

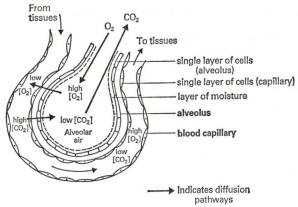

Fig. 4.13 Gas exchange at the alveolus

The sequence of events is as follows:

1 oxygen in alveolar air dissolves in moisture lining alveolus;
2 oxygen diffuses through single-celled alveolar and capillary walls into blood;
3 oxygen combines with haemoglobin in red blood cells to form oxyhaemoglobin (*see* p87);

4 carbon dioxide, transported as bicarbonate ions in blood diffuses through capillary and alveolar walls into moisture layer;
5 carbon dioxide diffuses from moisture layer into alveolar air.

Alveolar air composition remains nearly constant despite continual loss of oxygen to blood and gain of carbon dioxide, because diffusion occurs between it and tidal air which constantly brings in oxygen and removes carbon dioxide.

Table 4.4 Approximate composition of gases in breathed air

	Inspired air	Expired air	Alveolar air
Oxygen	21%	16%	14%
Carbon dioxide	0.04%	4%	6%
Nitrogen	78%	78%	80%
Water vapour	Variable	Saturated	Saturated

Experiment *To investigate changes in the composition of air during breathing in man.*

Apparatus

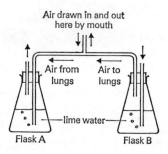

Fig. 4.14

Method The apparatus was set up and used as shown in Fig. 14. Breathing continued for 2 minutes.

Result The limewater in flask A was very milky. There was only a slight milkiness in flask B.

Conclusion Expired air contains more carbon dioxide than inspired air.

Respiration

Experiment *To investigate the gas produced by a small mammal during respiration.*

Apparatus

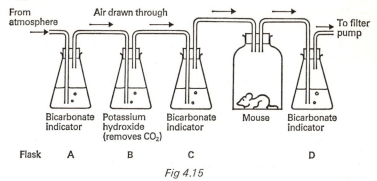

Fig 4.15

Method The apparatus was set up as in the diagram. Bicarbonate indicator is used to show changes in carbon dioxide levels in the flasks as follows:

$$\text{yellow} \xleftrightarrow{} \text{red} \xleftrightarrow{} \text{purple}$$
as CO_2 added — normal CO_2 level in atmosphere — as CO_2 removed

The bicarbonate indicator in all flasks was red at the beginning of the experiment.

Flask A tests the carbon dioxide level of atmospheric air.
Flask B removes carbon dioxide from air.
Flask C tests the carbon dioxide level of air passing to mouse.
Flask D tests the carbon dioxide level of air passing from mouse.
Air was passed through the apparatus for 15 minutes.

Results The original red colours of the bicarbonate indicator solutions were now:

Flask A	Flask C	Flask D
red	purple	yellow

Conclusions Flask C shows that air passing to the mouse contains less carbon dioxide. The result from flask D shows that the mouse has produced carbon dioxide as a waste product of respiration.

Gas exchange at tissues

Oxygenated blood passes from the lungs to the heart via the pulmonary veins. The heart distributes blood around the body to the tissues.

Diffusion of gases occurs throughout the body wherever a concentration gradient exists between the blood, tissue fluid and cells. In regions of low oxygen and high carbon dioxide concentrations oxyhaemoglobin releases its oxygen. This diffuses into the tissue fluid and then into the cells to be used in cell respiration. Waste carbon dioxide passes back into the blood down its concentration gradient and dissolves in the plasma forming bicarbonate ions.

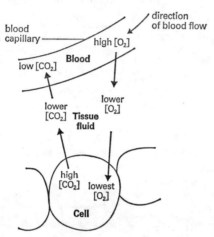

Fig. 4.16 Gas exchange at the tissues

Use the diagrams and notes given in this chapter to answer this question.

With the aid of diagrams, explain how, in a mammal, oxygen (a) reaches the lungs, (b) enters the blood stream and (c) is transported to the liver.
[12, 8, 5]   (LOND)

Gas exchange in flowering plants
The overall exchange of gas depends upon the light conditions.

During daylight Flowering plants carry out **photosynthesis** and **respiration.** The rate of photosynthesis is much greater than respiration and supplies all the oxygen for energy release and uses up the waste carbon dioxide from respiration. Gas exchange with the environment involves the uptake of carbon dioxide and release of oxygen.

During darkness Plants carry out respiration only. They take up oxygen and release carbon dioxide.

Comparison of photosynthesis and respiration

In many ways the two processes are opposite. Photosynthesis traps and stores energy whereas respiration releases the stored energy as shown below.

$$\text{carbon dioxide} + \text{water} \underset{\text{respiration}}{\overset{\text{photosynthesis}}{\rightleftharpoons}} \text{glucose} + \text{oxygen}$$

with **energy** (light) input and **energy** (chemical and heat) output.

All plants and animals respire at all times.
Green plants photosynthesize during daylight hours only.

List the differences between photosynthesis and respiration. (LOND)

Experiment *To investigate gas exchanges in plants during respiration and photosynthesis.*

Apparatus

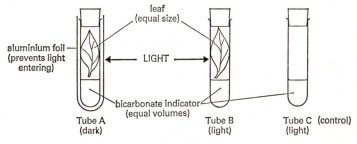

Fig. 4.17

Method Three boiling tubes were set up as shown and left for 2 hours (*see* p79 for details of bicarbonate indicator).

Results

Time (h)	Tube A	Tube B	Tube C
0	red	red	red
2	yellow	purple	red

Conclusion The control (C) shows that changes in colour of the bicarbonate indicator result from reactions occurring in the leaves. Photosynthesis was prevented in tube A by the absence of light. Carbon dioxide was produced in tube A by respiration. Photosynthesis and respiration occur in tube B but the rate of photosynthesis is greater than respiration.

Compensation point

At two points every 24 hours, gas exchange appears to cease. These are the compensation points and represent the times at which the rates of

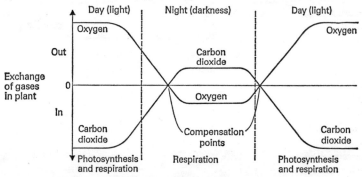

Fig. 4.18 Graph comparing photosynthesis and respiration

photosynthesis and respiration are equal (Fig. 4.18). Gas exchange in flowering plants occurs through openings called stomata and lenticels.

Stomata Tiny pores in the epidermis of leaves and soft green stems of herbaceous plants. The sequence of gas exchange is shown in Fig. 4.19.

Fig. 4.19 Gas exchange at the stoma   *Fig. 4.20* Lenticels

1 and 2 Oxygen diffuses in through stoma and into intercellular spaces.
3 Oxygen dissolves in moisture surrounding cell and diffuses into cytoplasm.

4 Oxygen used in respiration – maintains concentration gradient.
5 and 6 Carbon dioxide produced by respiration diffuses out along concentration gradient.

Lenticels Small openings in bark of woody stems filled with loosely packed cork cells and having many intercellular air-spaces (Fig. 4.20). Oxygen and carbon dioxide are exchanged here down their concentration gradients.

Key words

energy	cell membrane	ribs
aerobic	spiracles	intercostal muscles
glucose	tracheae	diaphragm
oxygen	tracheoles	pharynx
carbon dioxide	ventilation	larynx
water	gills	trachea
mitochondria	gill slits	epiglottis
ATP	opercular cavity	bronchi
metabolic rate	operculum	bronchiole
anaerobic	gill arch	alveoli
fermentation	filaments	pleural membrane
ethyl alcohol	lamellae	inspiration
lactic acid	epidermis	expiration
oxygen debt	lungs	photosynthesis
gas exchange	thoracic cavity	compensation point
diffusion	sternum	stomata
gas exchange surface		lenticels

Past examination questions

1 (a) *In the process of respiration living organisms can release and use chemical energy within a carbohydrate molecule.*
   (i) *Write an equation, in words or symbols, to show the beginning and end products of respiration when oxygen is freely available.*
   (ii) *Write an equation in words or symbols, to show the beginning and end products of respiration in one situation where oxygen is not available.*
   (iii) *What happens in active muscle tissue when the oxygen supply is temporarily insufficient?*

(b) Briefly explain why energy is needed (i) to make protoplasm, (ii) to circulate blood, (iii) to return essential salts from kidney tubules to blood.
(c) Energy is lost from plants and animals in the form of heat. Describe an experiment which shows that germinating seeds give off heat. (AEB)

2 Write a brief essay on the importance of respiration in plants and animals. (CAM)

3 Distinguish between respiration and ventilation (breathing). [6] (O)

4 Describe briefly how insects and flowering plants exchange respiratory gases. [6] (O)

5 Describe how oxygen is taken from the surroundings into the body of (a) a terrestrial insect, (b) a bony fish, and (c) a mammal. (CAM)

6 When the diaphragm muscles are relaxed, the central region of the mammalian diaphragm is
A approximately flat
B domed towards the thorax
C domed towards the abdomen
D domed ventrally towards the abdomen. (CAM)

7 The products of anaerobic respiration are energy and
A carbon dioxide and water
B glucose and water
C oxygen and acetic acid
D yeast and water
E alcohol and carbon dioxide. (LOND)

8 Describe (i) an experiment to show that germinating seeds evolve heat, and (ii) another experiment to show that they give off carbon dioxide. [7] (LOND)

5 Transport

Translocation Movement of substances about the plant.
Transpiration Loss of water vapour to the atmosphere from the surface of the plant.

All living organisms require a continuous exchange of materials between their cells and the environment, e.g. oxygen, carbon dioxide, water, food and waste products. Special structures on their surfaces allow these exchanges to occur. In single celled organisms, e.g. *Amoeba* and *Spirogyra*, movement of materials by diffusion and osmosis across the cell membrane supplies the needs of the organism. This also applies to multicellular animals where the tissue layers are thin, e.g. *Hydra*.

As organisms increase in size and complexity so do the distances between parts of the body and between internal tissues and the environment. Movement of materials within those organisms therefore requires a specialized transport system linking all the cells to the environment.

Transport in animals

The components of an efficient circulatory system are

1 a system of closed vessels (arteries, veins and capillaries);
2 a pump (the heart);
3 a circulatory fluid (blood).

Blood consists of about 55% fluid plasma and 45% cells. **Plasma** is a straw-coloured fluid consisting largely of water, with dissolved substances:

(a) salts – bicarbonates, phosphates, chlorides, sulphates, of sodium, calcium, potassium;
(b) food substances – mainly glucose, fats and amino acids;
(c) blood proteins – albumen, globulin and fibrinogen;
(d) excretory substances, mainly urea;
(e) hormones circulating from the glands which secrete them.

Blood cells
Red blood cells (erythrocytes)
Minute, biconcave disc-shaped cells (5 million per mm^3 blood) containing haemoglobin which carries oxygen from lungs to tissues. Shape and size gives them a very large surface area/volume ratio, ideal for rapid exchange of oxygen with the plasma. They have no nucleus and consequently a short life-span of about 3 months. They are destroyed by the liver and constantly replaced by cells in the bone marrow.

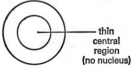

Fig. 5.1 A red blood cell

White blood cells (leucocytes)
Table 5.1 Types of white blood cell

White blood cells	Site of formation	Nucleus	Cytoplasm	Function
(a) **Lymphocyte**	Lymph nodes	Round	No granules	Release of antibodies
(b) **Granulocyte**	Bone marrow	Lobed	Contains granules	Phagocytic
(c) **Monocyte**	Bone marrow	Kidney-shaped	No granules	Phagocytic

Fig. 5.2 Types of white cell

There are about 8 000–10 000 white cells per cm^3 blood. They play a vital part in the defence of the body against disease.

Platelets (thrombocytes)
These are very small fragments of cytoplasm without a nucleus. They are formed in the bone marrow and are vital for blood clotting.

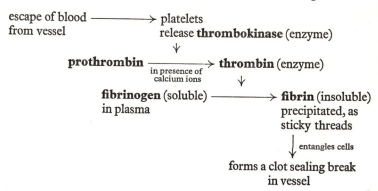

Functions of blood
1 Transport
(a) Oxygen from the lungs to the tissues. The red blood cells contain **haemoglobin** which picks up oxygen from the air in the lungs (*see* p77).

$$\text{haemoglobin} + \text{oxygen} \rightleftharpoons \text{oxyhaemoglobin}$$

Oxygenated blood containing oxyhaemoglobin is carried to the tissues. Here, the lower oxygen concentration and high carbon dioxide concentration causes the unstable oxyhaemoglobin to give up oxygen to the cells.

Haemoglobin is a respiratory pigment, and because of its affinity for oxygen, it increases the amount of oxygen the blood can carry.

(b) Carbon dioxide from the tissues to the lungs (*see* p77).
(c) Absorbed food (glucose, fats, amino acids) from the intestine to the tissues.
(d) Waste products from the tissues (e.g. urea from the liver) to the kidneys.
(e) Hormones from endocrine glands to the tissues on which they act.

2 Homeostasis
The blood temperature, osmotic pressure, acidity and levels of substances such as sugar, hormones and salts, are kept at constant levels by the various processes of homeostasis. Thus the body tissues are supplied with a fluid of constant composition.

3 Temperature regulation
  (a) The blood distributes heat from active organs which release much heat (liver, muscles), to the rest of the body.
  (b) By variation in the amount of blood flowing to the skin the amount of heat lost from the body can be changed according to the body temperature and external conditions (*see* p114).

4 Defence against disease
  (a) Phagocytic action of white cells.
  (b) Antibodies produced from lymphocytes (*see* p94).
  (c) Clotting (*see* p87).

Name six substances which are normally carried in solution in mammalian blood. [6] (O)

Blood groups
Human blood can be any one of four types depending on the presence or absence of two substances A and B on the red blood cell membranes. Other substances called Anti-A and Anti-B circulate in the plasma and can cause red cells to stick together in clumps if blood from different groups is mixed. A and Anti-A never occur together naturally. The features of each blood group are shown in Table 5.2.

Table 5.2 Blood groups in man

Blood group	Substance on cell	Substance in plasma
A	A	Anti-B
B	B	Anti-A
AB	A and B	Neither Anti-A nor Anti-B
O	Neither A nor B	Anti-A and Anti-B

Blood groups are genetically controlled (*see* p191).

Circulation of the blood
The heart
The **heart** is a four-chambered muscular pump, forcing blood round a closed system of vessels. Valves ensure that blood flows in only one

direction. The simplified diagram (Fig. 5.3) shows the basic features of the heart. This is a useful diagram for remembering structural relationships. An accurate fully-labelled drawing of the heart should be learnt – you may be expected to draw or label one.

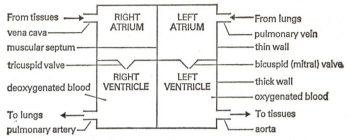

Fig. 5.3 Mammalian heart (diagrammatic representation)

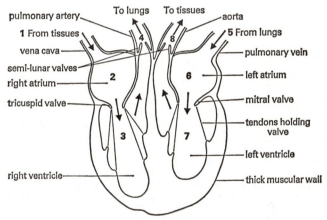

Fig. 5.4 Mammalian heart

Action of the heart (cardiac cycle)

The heart contracts rhythmically at an average of 70 beats per minute. Both auricles (atria) beat at the same time followed by both ventricles. The sounds of the heart beat are caused by the closing of valves produced by changes in pressure in the blood as the heart beats. The thick muscular walls of the ventricles produce a high pressure in the blood in the arteries leaving them. The functions of the various parts are annotated in Fig. 5.3 and the path taken by blood during the cardiac cycle is shown by the numbers in Fig. 5.4.

The structure of the heart and the cardiac cycle is well worth learning – it is a very popular question with examiners and often appears on short answer or objective test papers.

Blood vessels

There are three main types of blood vessels. You should be familiar with their structural similarities and differences and their functions within the circulatory system.

Table 5.3 Comparison of arteries, veins and capillaries

Arteries	Veins	Capillaries
Wall thick	Wall thin	Wall one cell thick
Thick muscle layer	Thin muscle layer	No muscle
Elastic fibres	No elastic fibres	No elastic fibres
Carry blood away from heart	Carry blood towards heart	Link artery and vein
Blood flow rapid	Blood flow slow	Blood flow slowing
Low volume	Increased volume	High volume
High pressure	Low pressure	Falling pressure
No valves	Valves present	No valves
Pulse	No pulse	No pulse
Blood oxygenated (except pulmonary artery)	Blood deoxygenated (except pulmonary vein)	Mixed oxygenated and deoxygenated blood

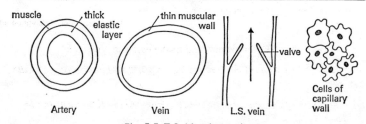

Fig. 5.5 T.S. blood vessels

Arteries break up into **arterioles** which lead to **capillaries**. These lead to **venules** which join up to form **veins**. The elastic walls of the arteries convert the irregular blood flow from the heart into a steady flow to the tissues. The capillaries are the site of exchange of substances between the blood and the tissues. Blood is returned to the heart in

Transport 91

veins by pressure produced by contraction of the skeletal muscles pressing on them from outside, and by breathing movements.

Use the information given above to answer the following question.

List four ways, either structural or functional, in which arteries differ from veins. [2]   (JMB)

The main blood vessels of the circulatory system are shown in Fig. 5.6.

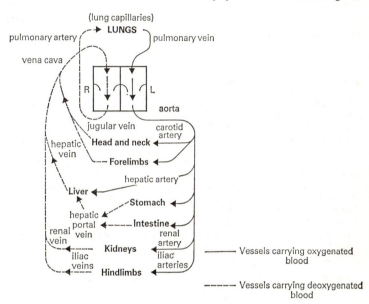

Fig. 5.6 Circulation and main vessels in a mammal

For each of the functions A–D select the appropriate blood vessel from the list 1–6.

A Transport of the products of digestion from the small intestine to the liver.
B Transport of oxygen from lung to heart.
C Transport of carbon dioxide from heart to lung.
D Transport of urea from liver to vena cava.

1 *Pulmonary vein*   4 *Hepatic portal vein*
2 *Pulmonary artery*   5 *Hepatic artery*
3 *Dorsal aorta*   6 *Hepatic vein* [2]   (JMB)

Exchange of substances between the blood and the tissues

In mammals all living cells are bathed in a fluid called **tissue fluid**. It forms a link between the blood and the cells. Materials (substances) moving between them must pass through tissue fluid but can only enter and leave the circulatory system through capillaries. (Why? *See* Table 5.3.)

Tissue fluid is formed at the arterial end of the capillaries where the high blood pressure forces fluid out through the thin walls of the capillaries into spaces between the cells. It is similar to plasma in containing oxygen, glucose and amino acids but does not contain protein molecules because they are too large to pass through capillary walls. The cells absorb oxygen and food by diffusion and active transport, utilize them and pass waste products (and some protein) out into the tissue fluid.

At the venous end of the capillaries, some fluid flows back through the capillary walls carrying carbon dioxide and waste from cells into the blood (*see* p80).

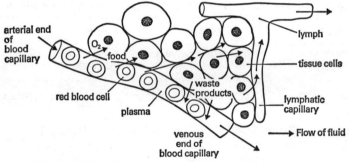

Fig. 5.7 Exchange of substances between blood and tissues – formation of lymph

Formation of lymph Not all the fluid which leaves the capillary is returned to the bloodstream. Some filters into small lymph capillaries and becomes **lymph**.

Composition of lymph It is similar to tissue fluid but contains some protein molecules. It is a watery solution of salts, sugars, amino acids, and contain proteins, fat droplets and some white blood cells, mainly lymphocytes.

Lymphatic system A system of vessels containing lymph supplies all parts of the body. The larger lymphatic vessels are similar to veins in structure and contain valves to direct the flow of lymph. At intervals along the vessels, lie **lymph glands** or nodes in which the lymph flows through narrow channels lined with phagocytic cells. These ingest and destroy any bacteria present in the lymph. Lymph nodes often occur in groups, e.g. in the neck and abdomen. Other areas of lymphatic tissue occur in the tonsils and intestinal lining. The **lacteals** of the villi are part of the lymphatic system (*see* p56). All lymph drains into two main lymphatic ducts which join the veins of the neck where the fluid, originally filtered from the blood, is returned to it.

Functions of lymphatic system
1 Transfer of substances between tissues and blood
2 Absorption of fat
3 Destruction of bacteria by phagocytes
4 Production of lymphocytes in lymph nodes
5 Antibody production by lymphocytes

Table 5.4 Differences between blood plasma, tissue fluid and lymph

Blood plasma	Tissue fluid	Lymph
Blood proteins	No blood proteins	Some proteins
Fat droplets	No fat droplets	Fat droplets

Questions on the lymphatic system are frequently asked in examinations, e.g.

1 *Give one difference between lymphatic fluid and blood plasma.* [1]
  Give two functions of the lymphatic system in mammals. [2]   (JMB)
2 *Lymph collects continuously in the tissue spaces surrounding the capillaries. How is it returned to the blood?*   (AEB)

Defence of the body against disease
1 The prevention of entry into the body of disease organisms (**pathogens**) is by
   (a) impermeable epidermis of skin;
   (b) healthy mucous membranes of nose and throat;
   (c) cilia lining nose and trachea;
   (d) bacteriocidal fluid in tears and nasal secretions;
   (e) clotting of the blood.
2 The destruction of organisms occurs when
   (a) acid in gastric juice kills bacteria;

(b) phagocytic cells ingest bacteria – lymph nodes; granulocytes and monocytes of blood; cells in liver and spleen;
(c) through immunity.

Immunity The ability to resist pathogens may be active or passive. **Active immunity** involves the production by the organism of antibodies. Pathogenic organisms entering the body act as **antigens**. They stimulate lymphocytes to produce and release specific chemical substances called **antibodies**. These react with the antigen and destroy it or neutralize its effects. The ability to produce this antibody at a later date protects against a second attack by the same pathogen.

This natural immunity can be supplemented artificially in some cases by immunization and vaccination. **Immunization** is the introduction of antigens into the body by mouth or injection. Attenuated (weak) pathogens, heat killed pathogens or toxoids (destroyed bacterial toxins) may be used as antigens.

Vaccination is a more effective and permanent form of immunization, e.g. measles, smallpox.

Passive immunity results from the organism containing antibodies derived from another organism, e.g. via placenta from mother to foetus, or injection of serum. It provides only short-term immunity but is useful in preventing epidemics.

What defence mechanisms are there in the body to combat the effects of pathogenic (disease-causing) micro-organisms? [12]   (o & c)

Transport in plants

The vascular bundles (*see* p21) are responsible for **translocation** of substances about the plant. The **xylem** (*see* p21 for structure) carries water and dissolved mineral salts from the roots to the leaves. The **phloem** (*see* p21) carries organic materials, mainly sugars and amino acids, from the leaves to growing points and storage organs.

Water transport
Transpiration

The loss of water vapour occurs mainly from the leaves of a plant. The lamina of a leaf is covered by a waterproof cuticle, so nearly all water loss occurs through gaps in the cuticle, the **stomata** shown in Fig. 5.8 (*see also* p27). Water evaporates from moist cell surfaces into the air in the sub-stomatal air space which becomes saturated with water vapour. Any factors producing a concentration gradient between the air spaces and the atomsphere will cause a continuous loss of water vapour through the stomata.

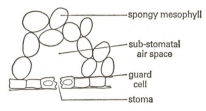

Fig. 5.8 V.S. stoma

Factors affecting transpiration

1 Atmospheric conditions, e.g. wind, high temperature, low humidity, increase rate.
2 Plant factors, e.g. surface area of leaves, number of stomata and whether open or closed.
3 Water supply.

Explain why the rate of transpiration increases when external conditions are changed from (i) humid to dry; (ii) cool to warm; (iii) still to windy; (iv) dark to light. (AEB)

Experiment *To investigate the effect of atmospheric conditions on transpiration rate.*

Apparatus

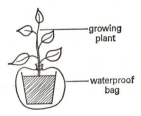

Fig. 5.9

Method A well-watered potted plant was set up as shown in Fig. 5.9. The plant was systematically left under conditions of high and low light intensity, wind, temperature and humidity for 3 hours. The plant was weighed before and after this period in each case and the results recorded.

Results The weight of water lost for high values of light, wind and temperature was greater than for low values. In the case of humidity, weight loss was lower for the high humidity value.

Conclusion Assuming that all weight losses were due to loss of water vapour then transpiration increases with rising light, wind and temperature levels and decreases with rising humidity. Increase in weight due to photosynthesis is relatively small and may be ignored.

Transpiration stream

When water is lost from the mesophyll cells, their cell sap becomes more concentrated and this increases their tendency to take in water.

Water passes by osmosis (*see* p29) from neighbouring cells into them. These cells in turn draw water from their neighbours, and in this way water passes across the leaf from the xylem vessels of the veins to the stomata.

The xylem forms a continuous system through the leaves, stem and root of the plant. When water is withdrawn from the xylem in the leaf, water passes up the vessels of the stem and root in a continuous stream. Such long narrow columns of water can remain unbroken because of the large forces of attraction between the molecules of water, and between the water and the sides of the vessels.

Experiment *To investigate the site of water transport in a stem.*

Method A plant shoot was cut off and left in a dilute solution of the red dye eosin for 3 hours. Transverse sections of the stem were cut and examined under the microscope.

Results The only tissue containing the dye and showing up red was the xylem.

Conclusion Water is transported through the stem in the xylem.

Water uptake by roots

Near the tip of the root the water passing along the xylem is replaced by water from neighbouring cells. This loss of water increases the osmotic potential of their sap, and they draw water from neighbouring cells. Water passes across the root through successive cells of the cortex until finally it is drawn from the **root hair** (*see* p22). Loss of water from the root hair causes water to enter it from the soil if it is available.

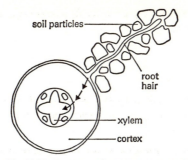

Fig. 5.10 Passage of water across root

Water passes from soil to air through the following parts of a plant: cortex, mesophyll, stoma, xylem, root hair, intercellular space.
(a) Rearrange the order of the above parts to show the route of water from soil to air. (AEB)

Root pressure is a force generated by the root of a plant and uses energy. It causes water to rise up the stem particularly in spring when

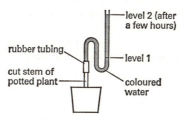

Fig. 5.11 Demonstration of root pressure

the absence of leaves on a tree means that there is no transpiration. If the stem of a potted plant, e.g. a vine, is cut off, and a manometer fitted as in Fig. 5.11, root pressure may be measured after a few hours.

Factors affecting water uptake
1 Rate of transpiration (which depends upon other factors, *see* p95)
2 Temperature
3 Osmotic potential of soil water
4 Availability of soil water
5 State of turgor of plant
6 Root pressure

Some of these factors may be demonstrated by using a **potometer**.
NB This apparatus does not directly demonstrate transpiration, but water uptake.

Experiment *To investigate the effect of various factors on water uptake using a potometer.*

Apparatus

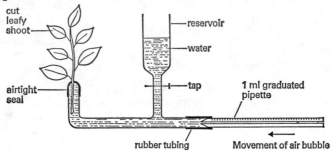

Fig. 5.12 The potometer

Method The stem of a leafy shoot was cut under water to prevent air entering the xylem. The apparatus was filled with water, and the shoot fixed into the open tube using rubber tubing and wax to make an airtight seal. The reservoir tap was closed and the apparatus left for 15 minutes to reach an equilibrium. An air bubble was introduced into the capillary tube and its passage timed along a specified distance on the scale. The reading was repeated until a steady result was obtained. The temperature was taken. Readings were repeated varying the conditions, e.g. high and low temperature; moving air; variation in humidity; darkness.

Results It was found that the rate of uptake was increased by high temperature, moving air, low humidity. It was decreased by low temperature, still air, high humidity and darkness.

Conclusions In general, conditions which affect transpiration rate will affect uptake in the same way.

What factors may affect the uptake by plants of water from the soil?
[8] (O & C)

Water loss from leaves

Since water loss occurs mainly through the stomata, it will be influenced by the state of opening of these pores. The stoma is guarded by two sausage-shaped **guard cells** with thickened inner walls. They are the only epidermal cells with chloroplasts.

When light is available for photosynthesis the concentration of sugar in the guard cells raises their osmotic potential, they take in water and become turgid. As the cell increases in volume the thickening on their inner walls causes the outer wall to curve more, opening the stoma. Therefore in light the stoma opens (Fig. 5.13(a)).

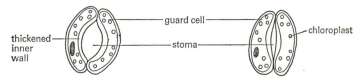

Fig. 5.13 Stoma (a) in the light, (b) in the dark

In the dark, the cell loses water, and the pore closes, cutting down water loss (Fig. 5.13(b)). It can be shown that water loss from a leaf is related to the presence of stomata, by using cobalt chloride paper. This is pale blue when dry and pink when wet. A small piece of the paper is

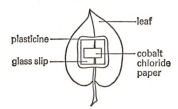

Fig. 5.14 Water loss from a leaf

enclosed under glass on both sides of a leaf (Fig. 5.14). It is found that it turns pink more quickly on the surface bearing stomata.

It can also be shown that water loss is faster through open stomata.

Uptake of mineral salts

Salts are absorbed in the form of **ions**, which are small particles carrying an electric charge. When in solution, a salt dissociates into two ions, one carrying a positive charge and one a negative charge. The plant may absorb one ion faster than the other depending on its needs (*see* p45).

Ions may enter the root by diffusion if there is a diffusion gradient into the root hair. Alternatively the root may absorb a particular ion by **active transport**, against the gradient. This process involves the use of energy produced in respiration, and is one reason why roots need oxygen.

After entering the root, the salts travel in dilute solution in water in the xylem, to the growing points, and to the leaves where they are necessary for protein synthesis. 'Ringing experiments' on stems, i.e. removing the bark and phloem (Fig. 5.15), show that the transport of salts is not affected. Therefore they must travel in the xylem.

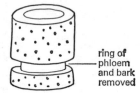

Fig. 5.15 'Ringing' a stem

Transport of organic materials

The movement of sugars and amino acids depends on the presence of living cells in the phloem. If the phloem is killed, translocation of organic material stops.

If a leaf manufactures carbohydrate in an experimental atmosphere containing radioactive carbon dioxide ($^{14}CO_2$) the radioactive sugar can be detected in the phloem both above and below the leaf. If the phloem below the leaf is killed by steam, the radioactive sugar can only be found above the leaf indicating that the dead phloem has lost the ability to conduct sugar.

If a stem is 'ringed' by removing a complete ring of phloem and bark the passage of organic materials up or down the stem is prevented. This can be shown by the presence of radioactive sugar on one side of the ring only. It cannot pass across the ring in the absence of phloem.

(a) *Describe an experiment to show that organic substances are translocated in the phloem of a deciduous tree.* [5]
(b) *Explain why it is better to carry out this experiment in summer rather than in winter.* [2]
(c) *Explain why fruit on a branch that has been ringed (a strip of tissue around the branch removed down to the wood) has unusually large fruits.* [3]
(d) *State three ways in which the transport system of a flowering plant differs from that of a mammal.* [3]   (JMB)

Key words

blood	pulmonary vein	antigens
plasma	left auricle	antibodies
erythrocytes	bicuspid valve	immunization
leucocytes	left ventricle	vaccination
lymphocyte	aorta	translocation
granulocyte	semi-lunar valves	xylem
monocyte	arteries	phloem
platelets	arterioles	vascular bundles
fibrinogen	capillaries	stomata
fibrin	venules	root hair
haemoglobin	veins	root pressure
heart	tissue fluid	potometer
vena cava	lymph	guard cells
auricles	lymph glands	ions
tricuspid valve	lacteals	active transport
right ventricle	immunity	
pulmonary artery	pathogens	

Past examination questions

1 (a) *One of the functions of the blood system of a mammal is to transport various substances, e.g. oxygen, around the body.*
    (i) *Name three other substances transported in the blood.*
    (ii) *How and where does oxygen enter the blood?*
    (iii) *How is oxygen carried in the blood?*
  (b) (i) *Name two tissues which transport substances in plants.*
    (ii) *Describe the nature, origin and destination of the substances carried by these two tissues.* (CAM)

2 *Urea is transported from the liver to the kidney in a mammal by the following parts of the blood circulation:*
  pulmonary vein, pulmonary artery, left auricle, right auricle, left ventricle, right ventricle, aorta, arterioles, venules, capillaries.
  (a) *Rearrange the order of the above parts to show the direct route of urea from the posterior (inferior) vena cava (which receives blood from the liver) to the renal artery (which takes blood to the kidney):*
  posterior vena cava → . . . → renal artery.
  (b) *Name two of the above parts where you would expect to find a high blood pressure.* (AEB)

3 *The drawings show three different components of blood.*

R   S   T

Complete the table by selecting the letter of the blood component which matches each description.

Description	Letter
essential for blood clotting	
can be produced in the lymphatic system	
produces antibodies	
there is a special need for iron in its production	

[2] (SCE)

4 *At a wound the platelets and cut blood vessels release the enzyme thrombokinase which, together with calcium ions and the soluble plasma protein prothrombin, forms the active enzyme thrombin. What happens next to form a blood clot?* (AEB)

5 *Explain how the circulatory system of a mammal performs its functions of (a) transport, and (b) defence.* [17, 8] (LOND)

6 *What substances are transported by (a) the blood system of a mammal, and (b) the vascular system of a flowering plant?*

    Briefly explain how (i) the flow of blood is maintained in a mammal, and (ii) the flow of water is maintained in a flowering plant. [25] (LOND)

7 *The cut end of an herbaceous stem was placed in a solution of eosin (a water-soluble red dye). A short time later a cross section of the upper part of the stem showed distinct red areas.*
  (a) Name the tissue which would have been stained.
  (b) Briefly describe what had happened to cause this staining. (AEB)

6 Excretion, osmoregulation and temperature regulation

Homeostasis The maintenance of a constant internal environment despite changes in the external environment.

Excretion The removal from the body of the waste products of cell metabolism. (Do not confuse with egestion or secretion.)

Metabolism The chemical processes occurring in living organisms.

Ultra-filtration The passage of small molecules from the capillaries of the glomerulus as a result of the high blood pressure within them. This process does not require energy.

Selective reabsorption The uptake of molecules required by the body, from the kidney tubules into the blood stream. Energy is required for this process.

Osmoregulation The process by which a constant balance of osmotic pressure is maintained in the body of an organism.

Homeostasis usually includes maintaining normal levels of salts, glucose, hormones, excretory products, pH value, osmotic pressure and, in birds and mammals, a constant body temperature.

The conditions under which cells work most efficiently are described as optimum. A change in pH or temperature may affect the enzymes in the cell and alter its metabolism. Each cell is responsible for its own 'internal environment' but it depends on a constant composition of the fluids surrounding it, to function normally. Maintenance of a constant internal environment is an active process and uses energy. Its advantage is that it makes the functioning of the body independent of changes in the external environment.

Excretion

The removal of waste products of **metabolism** is a vital part of homeostasis since it prevents the accumulation of substances which are toxic or would eventually interfere with the normal function of body cells.

Excretory products of animals

There are three main excretory products in animals, carbon dioxide, water and nitrogenous compounds.

Carbon dioxide and water are formed as a result of tissue respiration.

glucose + oxygen ⟶ carbon dioxide + water + energy

There are three excretory compounds containing nitrogen: **ammonia**, **uric acid** and **urea**. The form in which it is excreted depends upon the environment of the organism and how well it can control its water loss.

Ammonia Very toxic and very soluble. It is excreted as a dilute solution by those organisms with access to plenty of water, e.g. *Amoeba* and bony fish.

Uric acid Almost insoluble. Generally excreted as a white semi-solid, with very little water loss. Important in terrestrial organisms needing to conserve water, e.g. insects, reptiles and birds.

Urea Soluble, and relatively non-toxic. Excreted by dogfish and mammals.

Source of nitrogenous waste

All these compounds are derived from excess or unusable protein in the diet and from the breakdown of damaged and dead cells. This protein is broken down into amino acids and **deaminated** by the liver. The amino group ($-NH_2$) is removed from the amino acids and converted into one of the above forms as shown in the diagram below:

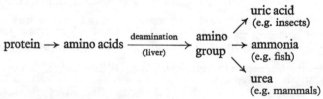

Most waste products containing nitrogen are toxic (poisonous) so must be eliminated quickly and efficiently.

Excretory organs

Protozoa Very small animals, like Protozoa, do not need a special excretory organ because their surface area is large in relation to their

Excretion, osmoregulation and temperature regulation

volume. This means that waste products can diffuse out of the body as quickly as they are formed, e.g. *Amoeba*.

Insects The excretory organs in insects are called **Malpighian tubules**. These long, fine tubules project from the gut and lie in the blood in the body cavity. They absorb nitrogenous waste from the blood and convert it into uric acid. The uric acid passes into the gut and is excreted as part of the faeces. These faeces therefore contain excreted and egested compounds.

Mammals

The main organs of excretion in a mammal are the **lungs, skin, liver** and **kidneys**.

Lungs Carbon dioxide is excreted by the lungs. It diffuses out of the blood into the air in the alveoli of the lungs and is breathed out with the expired air. Some water is lost in this way (*see* p78).

Name two substances excreted by the lungs. (CAM)

Skin Large quantities of sweat are secreted by the skin. The main purpose of this is loss of heat during evaporation, as part of the temperature regulating mechanism of the body. However, some excess water, salts and urea are excreted in the sweat.

In what ways is mammalian skin an organ of excretion? (LOND)

Liver Deamination of excess amino acids occurs here and urea is produced as described earlier. Another main function of the liver is the breakdown of old red blood cells. The haemoglobin in the cells is broken down to form **bile pigments**, excreted in the bile and lost from the body in the faeces.

Many candidates are confused over the organ where urea is formed and it is often asked in questions.

Where is urea formed in mammals? (A) liver, (B) pancreas, (C) kidney, (D) bladder. (CAM)

Kidneys The kidneys of a mammal excrete nitrogenous waste and are responsible for the osmoregulation of blood.

Structure and function of the mammalian kidney

The kidneys are two bean-shaped organs lying against the dorsal side of the abdominal cavity. They are dark red in colour because of the large amount of blood they contain. Each kidney is surrounded by a fibrous

capsule which maintains its shape. Three vessels join the kidney at the **hilum,** which is the indentation.

1 The **ureter** carrying urine to the bladder.
2 The **renal artery** carrying blood to the kidney.
3 The **renal vein** carrying blood away from the kidney (*see* Fig. 6.1).

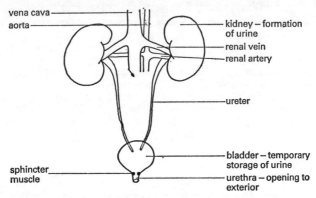

Fig. 6.1 The urinary system of a mammal

Kidney structure

Internally the kidney is divided into a darker outer **cortex** and a lighter inner **medulla**. In man, the medulla extends inwards to form 15–16 **pyramids**. The **collecting ducts**, which carry the **urine** towards the ureter, open into the **pelvis** at the tips of the pyramids (*see* Fig. 6.2). The urine is formed by the **nephrons** or kidney tubules (uriniferous tubules). There are about one million nephrons in each kidney in man. They lie mainly in the cortex.

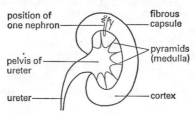

Fig. 6.2 V.S. kidney

Nephron Each nephron consists of a cup-shaped, hollow **Bowman's**

Excretion, osmoregulation and temperature regulation 107

capsule, and a long narrow tubule leading to a collecting duct (see Fig. 6.3). The tubule is divided into three regions with different functions: **1st convoluted tubule, loop of Henlé** and the **2nd convoluted tubule.** The nephron is supplied with blood at high pressure

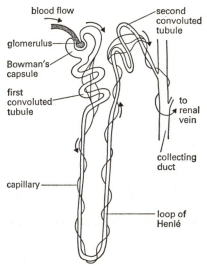

Fig. 6.3 A nephron

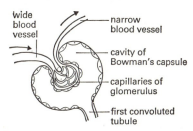

Fig. 6.4 Glomerulus and Bowman's capsule

by an **arteriole,** which breaks up into a knot of capillaries called a **glomerulus.** This lies in the cup of Bowman's capsule. Bowman's capsule and a glomerulus have walls only one cell thick (see Fig. 6.4).

It is important that you understand the *structure* of the kidney and nephron because only then can you fully appreciate how it functions.

Describe the structure of the kidney of a mammal and draw a labelled diagram to show an individual nephron (glomerulus and tubules) and its blood supply. [14]   (O & C)

Urine formation From the Bowman's capsule the arteriole breaks up into capillaries which twine round the nephron allowing reabsorption of substances to take place from the nephron to the blood. Urine formation takes place in two stages.

1 **Ultra-filtration** in Bowman's capsule. Blood runs to the glomerulus through an arteriole which is wider than the arteriole which leaves it. This produces a high blood pressure within the glomerulus. The blood pressure forces fluid and all dissolved substances with small molecules through the capillary walls of the glomerulus and into the cavity of Bowman's capsule. Proteins are too large to pass out of the blood. This fluid is called **glomerular filtrate.**

2 **Selective reabsorption** in other parts of the nephron. The glomerular filtrate flows along the narrow tubule of the nephron, and substances useful to the body are reabsorbed into the capillaries surrounding the tubule. The excretory materials and excess water left in the tubule are excreted as urine.

The regions of the nephron absorb different substances as shown in Table 6.1.

Table 6.1 Details of selective reabsorption

Region	Substances reabsorbed	Notes
First convoluted tubule	Glucose, amino acids, water	Uptake by **active transport** against concentration gradient Energy required
Loop of Henlé	Water	Important to terrestrial organisms
Second convoluted tubule	Water and salts	Regulation of blood pH and blood osmotic pressure according to water supply to organism
Collecting duct		

Use the information given above to answer this question.

Proteins and glucose are present in the blood which enters the kidney, but do not normally occur in the urine. For each one explain the mechanism

Excretion, osmoregulation and temperature regulation 109

which prevents it from appearing in the urine. (a) protein, (b) glucose.
[2] (SCE)

Urine
Man eliminates an average of 1500 ml of urine per day. This is mostly water (96%), urea and uric acid (2%) and sodium and potassium salts (2%). Urine passes out of the body as follows:

collecting ducts → pelvis → ureter → muscular bladder → **urethra**
(stored)   (during urination)

People suffering from a lack of the hormone, **insulin**, have an abnormally high level of glucose in their blood. They suffer from an illness called **diabetes mellitus**. The excess glucose is excreted by the kidney and appears in the urine (*see* p138).

Name four constituents of normal mammalian urine. (O)

Revision – functions of the mammalian kidney
1 Excretion of nitrogenous waste, mainly urea.
2 Elimination of excess amounts of normal substances from the blood, e.g. glucose.
3 Elimination of abnormal substances from the blood, e.g. alcohol, drugs, toxins in disease.
4 Maintenance of the pH of the blood.
5 Maintenance of the osmotic pressure of the blood.
6 Regulation of the salt content of the blood.
7 Elimination of hormones from the blood.

Excretion in plants
Plants make their own proteins by combining mineral salts, especially nitrates, with carbohydrates formed in the leaves during photosynthesis. They do not therefore have an excess of unwanted proteins because they only manufacture what they need. There is virtually no nitrogenous excretion in flowering plants.

Waste materials of metabolism can be eliminated as follows:

1 Carbon dioxide formed in respiration is used up during daylight in photosynthesis. During darkness it diffuses out of the leaf through the partially closed stomata.
2 Water formed in respiration may be used by the plant in photosynthesis. Excess is lost by evaporation from the stomata.

3 Oxygen is a product of photosynthesis. In daylight, the plant produces an excess of oxygen which diffuses across the leaf and out through the stomata to the atmosphere.
4 Some minor waste materials are deposited as solids inside cells.
5 In some deciduous trees waste is transferred to leaves in the autumn and lost when the leaves fall.

Information given on p105 and above can be used in answering the following type of question:

List the excretory products of (a) a mammal, and (b) a flowering plant.
(LOND)

Osmoregulation

A living cell is surrounded by a delicate membrane, the **plasmalemma**, across which osmosis may occur. Since the cell is easily damaged by either excess, or too little, water, it is vital that the fluid surrounding the cells should have a constant osmotic pressure. In very small organisms like *Amoeba* or *Hydra*, with no blood or tissue fluids, each cell must maintain its own osmotic balance.

In a large animal like a mammal there are special organs for the osmoregulation of the body as a whole.

Osmoregulation in protozoa

In *Amoeba*, living in fresh water, there is a tendency for water to enter the cytoplasm by osmosis through the partially-permeable cell membrane (*see* Fig. 6.5(a)). If uncontrolled, this would cause the *Amoeba* to swell and ultimately burst.

The amount of water in the cell is controlled by the **contractile vacuole**. Excess water collects in the contractile vacuole and is expelled

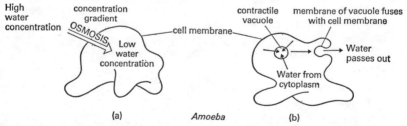

Fig. 6.5 Amoeba: (a) water entry by osmosis, (b) contractile vacuole

Excretion, osmoregulation and temperature regulation 111

at intervals through the cell membrane, thus maintaining the osmotic balance (*see* Fig. 6.5(b)).

Osmoregulation in mammals

The second convoluted tubule of the nephron in a mammalian kidney reabsorbs water from the fluid in the nephron into the blood. The amount of water reabsorbed and the concentration of urine varies according to the need of the body for water.

When the body is short of water more water is reabsorbed and less is excreted. When there is too much water in the body, the tubule absorbs less, and more water is lost in the urine. This variation in the amount of water lost in the urine maintains a constant water balance in the body. It is controlled by the secretion of varying amounts of **antidiuretic hormone** (ADH) by the pituitary gland. This hormone stimulates the second convoluted tubule to absorb water (*see* p137).

Temperature regulation

The largest organ in the body is the **skin** and one of its main functions in mammals is temperature regulation. Before considering this its structure should be fully understood.

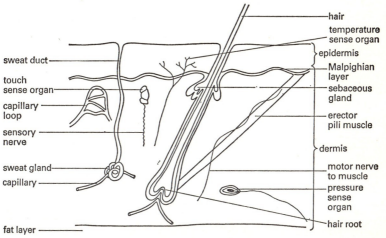

Fig. 6.6 Mammalian skin

A knowledge of Fig. 6.6 is important. Multiple-choice questions are often based on a given diagram but you may be asked to produce a diagram, e.g.

Make a labelled diagram of a vertical section through the mammalian skin. [6] (o)

The skin consists of two layers, the **epidermis** and the **dermis**.

Epidermis This is protective and is made up of stratified epithelial cells. These cells are continuously produced from the **Malpighian layer** which forms the boundary with the dermis. As new cells are produced, they move upwards through the epidermis because of the production of new cells from below.

A waterproof substance, **keratin**, is laid down in these cells which become more flattened and lose their nuclei, and finally die. They are eventually lost from the surface of the skin by friction. This constant replacement of cells is responsible for the ability of the skin to heal rapidly and to resist constant friction. The keratin waterproofs the epidermis preventing loss of water from the surface of the living tissues below.

The epidermis is pierced by pores which are the openings of sweat glands and by the hair follicles. In some mammals, most of the skin surface is covered by hair, which is insulating, and sometimes helps to camouflage the animals.

Dermis The dermis is the deeper layer of the skin containing hair follicles, blood vessels, sweat glands, muscles and nerves.

Hair follicles contain the shaft of the hair which is produced by the hair root at the base of the follicle. The upper part of the hair projects through the epidermis. Blood capillaries bring nourishment to the hair root.

Opening into the hair follicle from the side are **sebaceous glands** which secrete an oily fluid, **sebum**. This keeps the follicle free from dust and bacteria, and spreads as a thin film over the surface of the hair.

Attached to the base of the follicle is an **erector pili muscle**. This is attached to the underside of the epidermis at its other end, and when it contracts (shortens) it pulls the hair upright.

Sweat glands are coiled tubular glands lying in the dermis with a long slender duct which carries sweat to the opening (pore) on the surface of the skin. The water, salts and urea which make up sweat are brought to them by capillaries.

The blood vessels of the dermis bring nourishment and oxygen to the tissues and some play an important part in temperature regulation.

Excretion, osmoregulation and temperature regulation 113

There are many **capillary loops** just below the epidermis for this purpose (*see* Fig. 6.8).

Motor nerves stimulate the glands and muscles, and sensory nerves run from skin sense organs to the brain.

There are five types of sense organ in the skin, detecting heat, cold, touch, pain and pressure. Beneath the dermis is a layer of fatty tissue. This protects delicate organs from blows, and acts as an insulator.

Temperature regulation in mammals

Mammals and birds have a constant body temperature. They are said to be **homoiothermic**. All other animals are **poikilothermic**, i.e. their body temperature varies with that of the environment, and with their degree of activity (*see* Fig. 6.7).

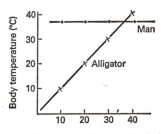

Fig. 6.7 Relationship between body temperature and environmental temperature in man and alligator

Advantages of a constant body temperature

1 Activity in animals depends on chemical changes (metabolism). Enzymes influence the rate of chemical change and are affected by temperature. A constant body temperature therefore allows animals to be equally active in winter, summer, day and night.
2 A constant body temperature makes an animal independent of the temperature of the environment. For example, polar bears, penguins and seals can inhabit very cold regions.

Control of body temperature

Maintenance of a constant temperature depends on balancing heat production and heat loss, so that

$$\text{heat lost from body} = \text{heat gained by body}$$

The hypothalamus in the brain controls temperature regulation. Nerves leave the hypothalamus and control the reactions of blood vessels, skin and muscles, to regulate heat gain and loss.

Heat production The source of body heat is tissue respiration. When carbohydrate is broken down in the cells to release energy for movement and other vital processes, about one third of the energy is released as heat. This heat is circulated around the body by the blood stream. The liver and muscles produce most heat, and the faster they work, e.g. during exercise and fever, the more heat they produce. Some heat is absorbed from the Sun.

Heat loss Heat is constantly lost from the skin by **convection**, **conduction** and **radiation**, and by evaporation of **sweat** from the skin and water from the lungs.

Some heat loss also takes place in expired air, faeces and urine. In man, in temperate regions, radiation is responsible for nearly half the heat loss from the skin. In very hot weather or strenuous exercise, sweating is more important.

Sweat glands are supplied by blood capillaries, from which they extract water, salts and urea which together form sweat. The water evaporates from the surface of the skin taking **latent heat** and so cooling the body. In furry animals, e.g. the cat, sweat glands are restricted mainly to bare areas such as feet.

Heat produced by cells is carried to the skin by the circulating blood. The blood vessels of the skin (**cutaneous**) play a vital part in temperature regulation. The blood flowing through them is cooled as heat escapes to the cooler air or water surrounding the animal.

Vasodilation When the capillaries are dilated (enlarged) the blood flow is increased, the skin becomes warm and red and more heat is lost.

Vasoconstriction When the capillaries are constricted (narrow) the blood flow is decreased, the skin becomes cool and pale and heat loss is

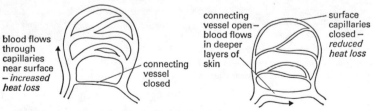

Fig. 6.8 (a) Vasodilation, (b) vasoconstriction

Excretion, osmoregulation and temperature regulation 115

reduced (*see* Fig. 6.8). A thorough understanding of the role of these blood capillaries is recommended.

As a result of vigorous exercise, the body of a man becomes hot and changes take place in the blood passing through the capillaries of the skin. Describe the changes and indicate their effects. (CAM)

Insulation

All homoiothermic animals have some form of insulation in or on the skin, to cut down heat loss.

Fat layer This is particularly thick in cold regions, e.g. blubber in whales in Antarctic seas.

Hair in mammals The air trapped between the hairs is a good insulator. A thicker coat traps more air and is therefore warmer. Furry animals have a thicker coat in winter.

The thickness of the fur layer can be increased by contraction of small muscles at the base of the hairs – pulling them upright, so that more air is trapped between them. In man, this causes 'goose flesh'. Beneath the outer feathers of birds there are many soft down feathers which trap air and so form a good insulating layer.

Regulatory mechanisms

A rise of body temperature above the normal value, e.g. in man 36.8 °C (98.4 °F) produces the following responses:

1 Increased sweating
2 Vasodilation – increased radiation, convection and conduction
3 Reduced muscular activity
4 Fewer clothes and reduced artificial heating
5 Hair lies flat against skin
6 Failure of above – heat stroke, **hyperthermia,** then heat death

A fall of body temperature below the normal value produces the following responses:

1 Sweating stops
2 Vasoconstriction – decreased radiation, convection and conduction
3 Increased muscular activity
4 Shivering – involuntary contraction of skin muscles
5 Additional clothing and artificial heating
6 Hair stands on end – 'goose flesh'
7 Failure of above – reduced 'core' temperature, **hypothermia,** then cold death

The following question usefully summarizes most of the main questions set on temperature regulation. Answer each part using the information given in the chapter.

Explain the following phenomena shown by the human body.
(a) *Violent exercise results in a rise in body temperature accompanied by noticeable sweating.* [5]
(b) *Shivering when we are cold.* [5]
(c) *Keeping cool in hot countries by wearing loose-fitting, light coloured clothing.* [5]
(d) *The formation of 'goose pimples' on the skin when cold.* [5]   (O & C)

Revision: functions of mammalian skin

1 Protection against – loss of water; entry of disease organisms; friction; ultra-violet light (melanin); and loss of heat (fat layer and hair).
2 Forms a flexible, slightly elastic covering for body, maintaining shape of body.
3 Temperature regulation by sweating, vasodilation and vasoconstriction.
4 Formation of vitamin D by action of sunlight.
5 Replacement of cells from Malpighian layer for rapid repair.
6 Contains sense organs of touch, heat, cold, pain and pressure.

Key words

homeostasis	renal	active transport
excretion	cortex	urethra
metabolism	medulla	insulin
ammonia	pyramids	diabetes
uric acid	collecting ducts	osmoregulation
urea	urine	plasmalemma
deamination	pelvis	contractile vacuole
Malpighian tubules	nephron	anti-diuretic hormone
lungs	Bowman's capsule	skin
skin	convoluted tubules	epidermis
liver	loop of Henlé	Malpighian layer
bile pigments	arteriole	keratin
kidneys	glomerulus	dermis
capsule	ultrafiltration	hair follicles
hilum	glomerular filtrate	sebaceous glands
ureter	selective reabsorption	sebum

Excretion, osmoregulation and temperature regulation 117

erector pili muscles
sweat glands
capillary loops
homoiothermic
poikilothermic

convection
conduction
radiation
sweat
latent heat

cutaneous
vasodilation
vasoconstriction
hyperthermia
hypothermia

Past examination questions

1 *Explain the origin and elimination of waste products in mammal and flowering plants.* [25]   (LOND)
2 *Some form of nitrogenous excretion occurs in all animals. Nitrogenous waste is usually in the form of urea, uric acid or ammonia.*
   (a) *Why is nitrogenous excretion insignificant in plants?* [3]
   (b) *In a single-celled animal such as Amoeba, the nitrogenous waste is usually ammonia. How would you expect this to be excreted?* [3]
   (c) *The table below shows the approximate compositions of blood plasma, urine and sweat in man.*

	Blood plasma g/l	Urine g/l	Sweat g/l
Water	910	960	990
Protein	74	0	0
Glucose	1	0	0
Urea	0.3	20	3
Salt (sodium chloride)	9	12	3

   (i) *Draw and label a single kidney tubule (a nephron) with its associated blood capillaries.* [5]
   (ii) *Explain the differences in concentration between blood plasma and urine of protein, glucose, urea and salt.* [4]
   (iii) *Draw and label a single sweat gland with its duct and associated blood capillaries.* [2]
   (iv) *Explain the differences in concentration between blood plasma and sweat of protein, glucose, urea and salt.* [3]
   (d) *Average urine production is 1.5 litre per day while average sweat production is 0.5 litre per day. In very hot surroundings as much as 5 litres of sweat may be lost in a day.*
      (i) *What changes would you expect in the volume and composition of urine in very hot surroundings?* [4]

(ii) *What changes in diet would be necessary to remain healthy in very hot surroundings?* [2] (AEB short answer)

3 *The main nitrogenous waste excreted by land mammals is urea. Freshwater fish excrete ammonia.*
   (a) *How is this difference in excretory products related to the environment of the two types of animals?*
   (b) *Freshwater fish take in much water because of osmosis. How must their kidneys differ in their functioning from those of a mammal in order to maintain the body fluids at a constant concentration?* (AEB)

4 *What would be the effect on the conditions and activities listed in the table below if a man drank a litre of water?*
Fill in the table using the words: increases, decreases, stays the same.

Condition/activity	Effect
osmotic pressure of the blood	
production of ADH*	
production of adrenalin	
concentration of the urine	
volume of the urine eliminated	

*antidiuretic hormone [3] (SCE)

Questions 5–8 refer to numbered structures in the following diagram of a mammalian kidney tubule (nephron).

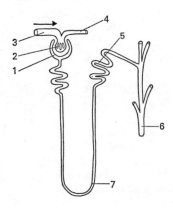

5 *Solutes pass from 2 to 1 due to*
  A *osmotic pressure*
  B *high pressure*
  C *diffusion pressure*
  D *active secretion*
  E *selective reabsorption.* (LOND)
6 *The fluid with the highest water content is found in*
  A 1
  B 4
  C 5
  D 6
  E 7. (LOND)
7 *Water is reabsorbed mainly at*
  A 1
  B 2
  C 3
  D 4
  E 7. (LOND)
8 (a) *Make a labelled diagram of a single nephron of a mammalian kidney.* [8]
  (b) *List the components of urine and explain fully how urine is produced.* [13]
  (c) *Which is the main nitrogenous excretory substance?* [1]
  (d) *In which organ is it formed?* [1]
  (e) *Give two important properties of this substance which make it suitable as an excretory material.* [2] (O)

7 Coordination

Irritability The ability, shown by living organisms, to respond to a stimulus.

Homeostasis The maintenance of a constant internal environment despite changes in the external environment.

Tropism A growth movement (response) by part of a plant in a direction determined by the direction of the stimulus.

Neurone A nerve cell.

Synapse The junction between one nerve cell and another or between nerve cell and effector.

Reflex action and **reflex arc** An involuntary response to a stimulus and the nerve pathway taken from receptor to effector in a specific reflex action.

Receptor A structure capable of converting a stimulus into an electrical impulse.

Effector A structure capable of converting electrical energy of a nerve impulse into a response.

Hormone A specific chemical substance produced in animals by an endocrine gland, it enters the circulatory system and passes to a cell, tissue or organ where it produces a specific response.

Gland A structure capable of secreting a chemical substance.

Behaviour The way in which an organism responds to a stimulus.

Taxis The movement of a whole organism in response to a directional stimulus.

Kinesis The change in rate of movement of an organism in response to the intensity of stimulus.

Irritability is a characteristic of all living organisms. It is the means by which they respond to stimuli in order to maintain the best conditions for life.

Coordination

Stimuli are produced by changes in the environment, e.g. sound waves, temperature change. Many stimuli are forms of energy. They are detected by specialized regions of organisms called receptors, which may be situated inside or outside the organism. **Receptors** detect stimuli and set up an electrical current which travels as a nerve impulse to an **effector** which produces the appropriate **response**.

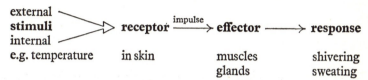

The type of response and its extent and duration are all directly related to the nature of the stimulus.

Coordination is the process whereby the organism makes the correct response at the correct time to the given stimulus. It has an important role in allowing the organism to adapt to change and increase its chances of survival. Mechanisms of coordination maintain the functioning of organisms at a constant level. These processes are therefore **homeostatic**.

Coordination in plants is controlled by hormones. In animals it is under the control of hormones and nerves.

Plant responses

This is a favourite topic with examiners so learn it very well, especially the experimental evidence and the explanation of phototropism and geotropism. A typical type of question on this topic is given below.

How do the shoots (or coleoptiles) of plants respond to light reaching them from one side only? Describe the mechanism by which these changes are brought about. (CAM)

This type of question may be answered by using the following information.

Plants respond to stimuli by the production and/or release of a chemical substance which functions as a hormone. These substances are involved in root and shoot growth, flowering, leaf-fall and produce the growth responses made to light and gravity. The commonest plant growth substances are called **auxins**, e.g. indoleacetic acid (IAA). They are produced at the apices (tips) of shoots and roots. They stimulate growth by increasing the rate of cell elongation in the region just behind the shoot tip. In the case of root tips auxins may inhibit growth.

The regions of sensitivity to stimulus and response can be demonstrated by the experiments shown in Fig. 7.1.

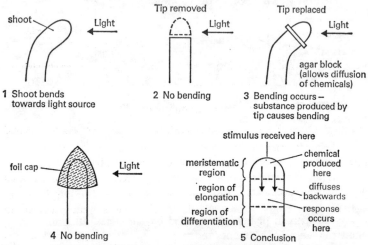

Fig. 7.1 Regions of sensitivity on a shoot

Plants respond to light, gravity, temperature, water, chemicals and touch. Most responses are bending movements produced by cell elongation in the growth region behind the stem or root tip.

Tropism
A tropic movement is a growth movement by part of a plant in a direction determined by the direction of the stimulus. This may be towards the stimulus (positive tropism), or away from it (negative tropism). The type of tropic movement depends upon the nature of the stimulus, e.g. positive phototropism – growth towards light.

Phototropism
This is a growth movement produced in response to light by most shoots (stems and coleoptiles). The normal response is positive phototropism, i.e. bending towards the light stimulus.

Experiment *To investigate the effect of light on germinating oat seedlings.*

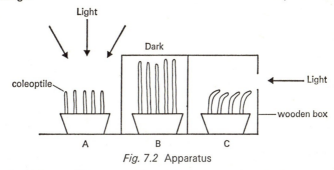

Fig. 7.2 Apparatus

Method Oat seedlings were planted in moist compost in three pots and set up in the apparatus above under the light conditions shown.

Results After 10 days the coleoptiles had grown as shown.

Conclusions Normal upward growth occurred in pot A due to equal illumination from above. Excessive growth occurred in pot B due to lack of light. Bending of the coleoptiles towards light occurred in pot C when illuminated from one side only.

Light either destroys auxins or causes them to accumulate on the dark side of the shoot. The above results can be explained by Fig. 7.3.

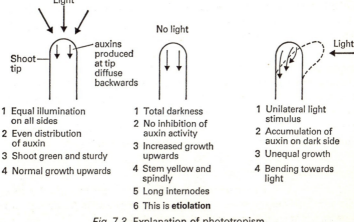

Fig. 7.3 Explanation of phototropism

Geotropism

This is a growth movement produced in response to gravity by shoots and roots. Shoots are negatively geotropic and roots are positively

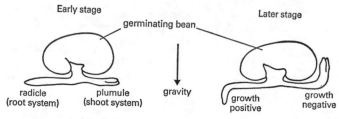

Fig. 7.4 Demonstration of geotropism

geotropic. These opposite growth effects may be explained in terms of the different responses shown by shoots and roots to auxins as shown in Fig. 7.5.

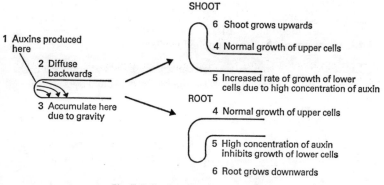

Fig. 7.5 Explanation of geotropism

A **clinostat**, by eliminating the effects of gravity, may be used to demonstrate that tropisms result from unilateral stimuli. Germinating seedlings are rotated slowly so that gravity exerts its effects on all sides of the root in turn. Their radicles grow horizontally. The radicles of seedlings grown in a control clinostat, which is not rotating, grow downwards. This shows that these growth movements are made in response to gravity.

Nervous system

In most animals this is composed of the central nervous system, **CNS** (brain and spinal cord) and the nerves connecting it to receptors (sense cells) and effectors (muscles and glands). This system allows coordination between stimulus and response.

The basic unit of the nervous system is the **neurone** (nerve cell). There are three types of neurones, **sensory**, **intermediate** and **motor**, sharing the same basic function of transmitting electrical impulses. They

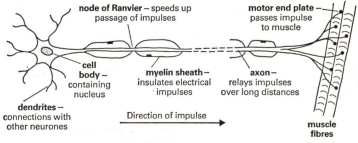

Fig. 7.6 Motor neurone

vary in structure and are found in different regions of the nervous system (*see* Fig. 7.7).

Nerve impulse and synapse

Information passes from receptor to effector along nerves. A **nerve** is a collection of **nerve fibres**. Information is transmitted as a nerve impulse. A nerve impulse passes along an axon at a very high speed as a weak electric current. At the ending of each neurone there is a gap called a **synapse** between it and the next neurone or an effector. When a nerve impulse reaches a synapse it causes the release of small amounts of a chemical substance called a **transmitter substance**. This either sets up a nerve impulse in the connecting neurone, causes contraction of a muscle effector or secretion by a gland. Some transmitter substances act as hormones, e.g. adrenaline.

Central nervous system

This is composed of the brain and spinal cord. All information from the external and internal environments passes through the CNS where reactions are coordinated.

Reflex arc and reflex action

The simplest form of reaction in the nervous system is reflex action. This is a rapid involuntary response to a stimulus and is not under the conscious control of the brain (involuntary action). The pathway taken by the nerve impulses in reflex action forms a reflex arc.

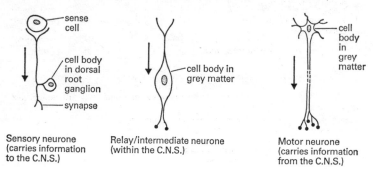

Fig. 7.7 Types of neurones

The basic pathway of a reflex arc is shown in Fig. 7.8 in the order in which reflex action is produced. Learn the basic principle and relate this

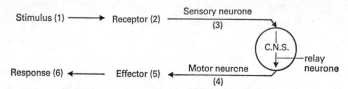

Fig. 7.8 Diagrammatic representation of the reflex arc

to the example given in Fig. 7.9. This shows the reflex arc involved in producing the response to pricking a finger on a pin.

Another good example is the knee jerk reflex but it does not have an intermediate (relay) neurone. In this case the sensory neurone synapses directly onto the motor neurone.

Questions on reflex arcs and action are common in examinations. It is worth checking that this topic is fully understood.

(a) *What is a reflex action?* [3]
(b) *Draw a large, clearly annotated diagram to show how reflex action is brought about in response to a painful stimulus.* [14]   (LOND)

Coordination 127

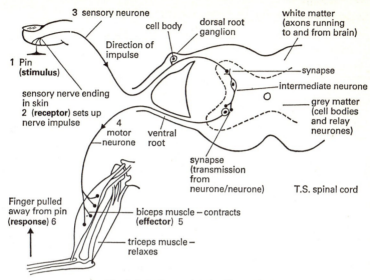

Fig. 7.9 Reflex arc and reflex action

An answer to each of these questions should include the information given above. Related questions are equally straightforward, e.g.

Why is it important for animals to have simple reflexes? [5]   (O & C)

Simple reflex arcs allow the body to make automatic adjustments (involuntary) to changes in (a) the external environment, e.g. iris – pupil reflex, balance during locomotion; (b) the internal environment, e.g. breathing rate, blood pressure, and to prevent damage to the body, e.g. cuts, burns.

Conditioned reflexes   These are reflex actions where the type of response is modified by past experience. **Learning** forms the basis of conditioned reflexes, e.g. toilet training, awareness of danger, conscience, salivation on sight and smell of food.

In animals with a well-developed central nervous system neurones send impulses from the sensory/intermediate synapse to the brain. Information stored here from past experiences allows a decision to be made concerning the nature of the response. Excitatory neurones carry impulses back to the motor neurone cell body of that reflex arc and a positive response is made. Inhibitory neurones prevent the automatic response from being made, e.g. a hot metal plate if picked up would be dropped whereas a boiling hot casserole would probably be put down quickly but gently.

Brain

This is the enlarged front end of the nerve cord in vertebrates. It acts as a reflex centre for reflex arcs in the head, involving the main sense organs, the eyes, ears, mouth and nose. The increased importance of these has led, during evolution, to an increase in the size and complexity of the brain. Most of the information entering the CNS passes through the

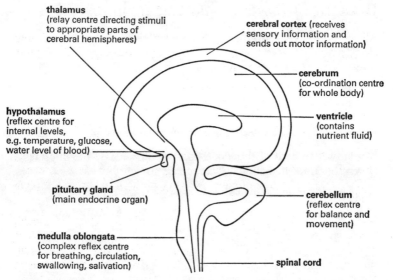

Fig. 7.10 Section through the human brain, with annotations

brain and it has control over most of the responses made by the body (voluntary action). It is an organ of coordination, memory, learning and reasoning and is highly developed in man.

It is unlikely that questions will be asked requiring a drawing of the brain – more likely you will be asked to label a diagram provided. The human brain has the following structure and functions (*see* Fig. 7.10).

The largest part of the brain is the **cerebrum** (cerebral hemispheres) which spreads out and covers most of the brain. It is concerned with collecting information from sense organs and storing it for later use (learning and behaviour). Reasoning, conscience, learning and personality are controlled by the cerebrum. The outer covering of the cerebrum is the **cerebral cortex** and various regions of it are concerned with specific senses, e.g. sight, hearing, touch, and the control of specific parts of the body, e.g. fingers, tongue, neck, and functions, e.g. speech. Information from many sense organs is collected together in certain parts of the cerebrum called **association centres**. Here sensory information is compared with similar past experiences and impulses are sent to effectors to produce the appropriate response.

Receptors (sense cells and organs)

All receptors have the same basic function of converting stimuli into electrical energy of the nerve impulse. There are three types of receptors named according to their position:

1 **exteroceptors** for detecting external stimuli, e.g. light;
2 **interoceptors** for detecting internal stimuli, e.g. blood temperature;
3 **proprioceptors** for detecting position and movement.

Receptors may be isolated single cells, e.g. pressure receptors in the skin, or collected together to form a highly efficient sense organ, e.g. the eye.

The strength of the stimulus determines the number of receptors sending impulses to the CNS.

Skin receptors The skin contains sense cells detecting heat, cold, touch, pressure and pain (*see* p111). Each of these types of cell is capable of responding to a range of strengths of stimuli so that the brain can register degrees of stimulation. Certain parts of the body are more sensitive to stimuli than others, e.g. tip of tongue and fingers and lips. In these areas each sense cell has its own nerve fibre running to the CNS. The skin may act as a receptor and effector in temperature regulation (*see* p114).

Muscles, joints and tendons These contain pressure receptors which relay information to the CNS about degree of stretching, tension and position. The brain correlates this information and can identify the position of the limbs. This information is required before accuracy of limb movement can be achieved.

Smell and taste Certain receptors detect chemical substances which dissolve in the film of moisture covering them. Taste receptors on the tongue are situated in taste buds and are sensitive to bitterness, saltiness, sourness and sweetness.

Eye

The structure of the human eye enables it to convert light rays of various wavelengths coming from varying distances into electrical impulses which nerves carry to the brain where an image of remarkable precision is produced.

When learning a diagram of the structure of the eye (Fig. 7.11) notice

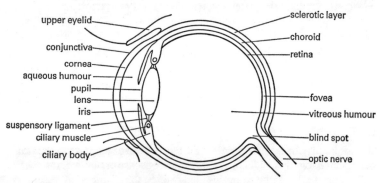

Fig. 7.11 The human eye

that the conjunctiva is joined to the eyelids, the cornea and sclerotic layer form a continuous ring; the choroid, iris, ciliary body and lens form another ring with the retina forming the inner lining.

Sclerotic layer (sclera) External covering of eye, very tough, maintains shape of eyeball.

Choroid Contains blood vessels – supplies nutrients to rest of eye, black pigment prevents reflection within eye.

Retina Contains sensory rods and cones.

Fovea Most sensitive part of eye, cones only, most light rays are focussed here.

Vitreous humour Clear, semi-solid substance supports eyeball.

Blind spot Point where optic nerve leaves eye – no rods or cones here, therefore not light-sensitive.

Optic nerve Bundle of nerve fibres carrying impulses to brain.

Eyelid Protects the eye from damage by reflex action.

Coordination 131

Conjuctiva Thin layer of transparent cells protecting cornea.
Cornea Transparent front part of sclerotic, curved surface with aqueous humour beneath acts as main structure refracting (bending) light towards retina.
Pupil Opening in iris – all light enters eye through here.
Iris Coloured, muscular diaphragm, adjusts amount of light entering eye.
Aqueous humour Clear watery fluid supports lens (*see* cornea).
Lens Transparent, elastic, final adjustment of focus of light rays.
Suspensory ligament Attaches lens to ciliary body.
Ciliary body Edge of choroid and contains the ciliary muscles
Ciliary muscles Circular muscles alter shape of lens during accommodation.

Light entering the eye takes the following path:
conjunctiva → cornea (where light rays are refracted for focussing onto retina) → aqueous humour → pupil → lens (precise focussing onto retina) → vitreous humour (*a* comes before *v* in alphabet – helps remember order of humours) → sense cells in retina.

Accommodation
This is the mechanism by which light rays from an object are focussed onto the retina so as to produce an image. It involves two processes.

1 Reflex adjustment of pupil size according to light intensity (in bright light the circular muscle of the iris diaphragm contracts, the pupil becomes smaller and less light enters the eye preventing damage to the retina, in shade the opposite happens).
2 Muscles in the ciliary body alter the shape of the lens according to the distance of the object from the eye.

Figure 7.12 may be used to help answer the following question.

Explain how the amount of light reaching the retina is regulated. [3]   (JMB)

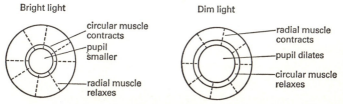

Fig. 7.12 The iris/pupil response to light

132 Biology

Figure 7.13 would be useful in answering questions of this type:
Give labelled diagrams and explain the functions of (a) ciliary muscles and suspensory ligaments of the eye in focussing. (LOND)

Light from distant object

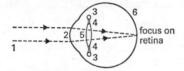

1 Parallel light rays reach eye
2 Cornea refracts (bends) light rays
3 Circular ciliary muscle relaxed
4 Suspensory ligament taut
5 Lens pulled out thin
6 Light focussed on retina

Light from near object

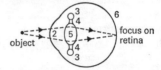

1 Diverging light rays reach eye
2 Cornea refracts (bends) light rays
3 Circular ciliary muscle contracted
4 Suspensory ligament slack
5 Elastic lens more convex
6 Light focused on retina

Fig. 7.13 Mechanisms of accommodation

Defects of vision and their correction

Information included in Fig. 7.14 may be used in answers to questions such as the one below.

Short sight (eyeball too long)
Without extra lens, distant objects focus in front of retina ---▶---
Corrected as shown ———▶———

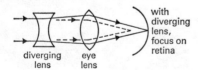

Long sight (eyeball too short)
Without extra lens, near objects focus behind retina ---▶---
Corrected as shown ———▶———

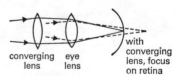

Fig. 7.14 Correction of vision defects

By means of two simple labelled diagrams, illustrate image formation in the eye of a short-sighted person when looking at a distant object (i) without corrective lenses, and (ii) with corrective lenses. [4] (JMB)

Coordination 133

Colour vision There are two types of sense cells in the retina, **rods**, which are sensitive to low-light intensities, and **cones**, which respond only to bright light. Cones detect colour and there are thought to be three types of cone cell in mammals, each responding to one of the primary colours, red, green and blue. Light of other colours and shades stimulate varying proportions of these cones. Impulses from these pass to the brain where the sensation of colour is produced. Nocturnal animals have many rods and few cones giving them better night vision but poor colour discrimination, e.g. owls.

Stereo-vision (binocular vision) This occurs when both eyes focus on the same object simultaneously. It enables distance and depth to be judged accurately. Man and predatory animals, particularly birds of prey, have well-developed stereo-vision since their eyes are placed in the front of the head.

Arthropod eyes Knowledge of this is not required by all examining boards, check first.

Simple eyes are found in some insects. These consist of a few light sensitive cells. They discriminate light and dark but do not produce images. Most insects and crustacea have compound eyes made up of thousands of separate structures called **ommatidia**. Each ommatidium is composed of a lens, pigmented cells (preventing internal reflection) and light sensitive cells which set up nerve impulses in the sensory neurones running from them. Each ommatidium produces a separate image in the brain, the overall effect being a mosaic image. This lacks the definition produced by the mammalian eye but is very sensitive to movement.

Ear
The mammalian ear is a sense organ involved with balance and hearing. Movements and positions of the head are detected by the semicircular canals, utriculus and sacculus. All other structures are involved in hearing.

Hearing
Sound travels as pressure waves and the pitch or frequency of the sound increases as the wavelength decreases. The ear can be divided into three sections each specializing in different functions.

1 **Outer ear** The **pinna** collects and focusses sound waves into the ear tube. This causes the **ear drum** (tympanic membrane) to vibrate.

134 Biology

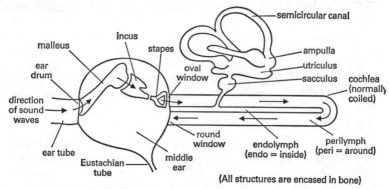

Fig. 7.15 Functional diagram of the human ear

2 **Middle ear** This contains air. Equal pressure on each side of ear drum is maintained by connection to pharynx by **Eustachian tube** – prevents rupture of the ear drum. Ear drum vibrations are amplified 22 times by the lever system of the three **ossicles** of the ear (malleus, incus and stapes) and transmitted to the **oval window**.
3 **Inner ear** Movements of the oval window set up vibrations in the incompressible **perilymph** of the **cochlea**. The **organ of Corti** is the structure in the cochlea which converts the mechanical energy of the sound waves into nerve impulses which pass to the brain by the **auditory nerve**.

Sensory hairs embedded in the rigid tectorial membrane pass to sense cells in the basilar membrane. Vibrations pass from the oval window along the upper chamber and back to the round window along the lower

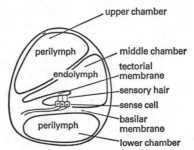

Fig. 7.16 T.S. cochlea showing organ of Corti

chamber. These vibrations cause the basilar membrane to move up and down and the hairs pull on the sense cells which set up impulses in the nerve fibres. The width of the basilar membrane increases with distance from the windows. Each frequency produces vibrations in a specific region of the membrane – high frequencies where the membrane is narrowest and low frequencies where it is wider. (In the piano, harp and other stringed instruments it is the length of string vibrating which produces the frequency and pitch of the sound.)

Balance

The **utriculus** and **sacculus** contain sensory cells which are stimulated by movements of objects called **otoliths**. An otolith is a gelatinous mass containing granules of calcium carbonate and hairs projecting from sense cells. Gravity always acts at right angles to the Earth's surface

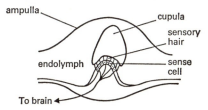

Fig. 7.17 Ampulla and cupula

and any movement of the head with respect to gravity is detected by otoliths.

The three semi-circular canals are arranged in three planes at right angles to each other and detect the direction and rate of change of position, of the head. Each canal has a swelling called an **ampulla** containing a **cupula,** which is a gelatinous structure containing sensory hairs attached to sense cells (Fig. 7.17). Movement of the head, semi-circular canals and cupula is resisted by the **endolymph** which remains stationary. This produces a relative displacement of the cupula which stimulates the sense cells and impulses pass to the brain.

Information from the eyes, muscles, joints and tendons passes to the brain which coordinates all this sensory information to maintain balance and equilibrium.

Effectors (muscles and glands)

These are cells or organs which produce a particular response when stimulated by motor neurones.

Muscles An example of a muscular effector system may be demonstrated by the bending of the fore-arm at the elbow (*see* diagrams on p150 and p127). Other examples are swallowing p54, accommodation p131 and peristalsis p54. Coordinated muscle effector systems are involved in movement of the whole organism in response to stimuli (*see* p139, taxes).

Glands Some motor neurones supply glands which respond by secreting substances such as enzymes (e.g. salivary glands), tears or mucus, whilst those supplying endocrine glands cause the secretion of hormones, e.g. pituitary gland.

Endocrine system

This works either separately or in conjunction with the nervous system to coordinate growth, development and activity within an organism. Hormones are released by glands (*see* definitions, p120).

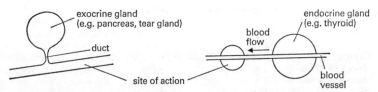

Fig. 7.18 Glands: exocrine (ducted) and endocrine (ductless)

There are two types of glands called **exocrine** and **endocrine** (Fig. 7.18). Questions testing understanding of the important terms given above are quite common, e.g.

Explain what is meant by the terms hormone and endocrine organ. (CAM)

Always be sure that terms such as these are well known.

The main endocrine glands in the body are the pituitary, thyroid, pancreas, adrenals and reproductive glands. The **pituitary gland** coordinates and controls the activity of the other glands by the release of hormones which stimulate them to produce or release their own hormones.

The level of circulating hormone is controlled by a process called **'feed-back'**. In this, the level of hormone in the blood is monitored as it passes through the brain. If too much is present the pituitary is prevented from releasing a stimulating hormone, if too little is present

Table 7.1 Summary of hormones

Gland/position	Hormone produced	Stimulus	Function
	Anti-diuretic hormone (ADH)	Dehydration	Reabsorption of water into blood from kidney tubule (p111)
	Oxytocin	Mature foetus	See p169
	Thyroid stimulating hormone (TSH)	Feedback	Release of thyroxine by thyroid gland
Pituitary (base of brain)	Corticotrophin (ACTH)	Feedback	Release of hormones from adrenal cortex
	FSH	Lack of progesterone	See p167
	LH	Oestrogen	See p167
	Growth hormone	Feedback and age	Increase rate of cell division and protein synthesis
Thyroid (neck on each side of larynx)	Thyroxine	TSH	Regulation of metabolic rate
Islets of Langerhans of pancreas (below stomach)	Insulin	Increased blood sugar level	Lowers blood sugar level, stimulates glucose uptake by cells
Adrenal medulla (above kidney)	Adrenaline	Danger, fright, stress	Increases heart and breathing rate, and blood flow to brain and muscles, raises blood sugar level, stops peristalsis
Adrenal cortex	Corticosteroids	ACTH	Regulates salt balance in blood
Ovary, uterus testis	See p167		

it releases even more. In this way a very precise control of hormone levels can be achieved to suit the varying needs of the organism. Table 7.1 is a summary for the topic of hormones. Knowledge of these glands, their hormones and their effects is frequently demanded on objective test papers. Learn the table.

In some important metabolic activities, hormones from several glands

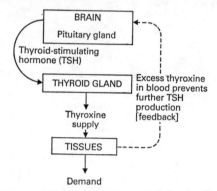

Fig. 7.19 Feedback control of thyroxine output

may be required to produce precise chemical coordination, e.g. the control of blood sugar level. Adrenaline and thyroxine raise the blood sugar level. Insulin lowers it. The control of glucose metabolism is shown in Fig. 7.20, where a = adrenaline, t = thyroxine and i = insulin.

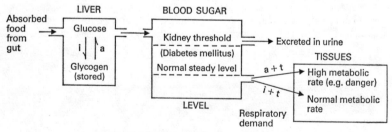

Fig. 7.20 Control of blood sugar level

This is a good example of a topic which requires details from various parts of the syllabus. List the processes shown on the diagram above and look them up in detail in other sections of this book.

Table 7.2 Differences between nervous and chemical coordination

Nervous	Chemical
1 Information passes as electrical impulses along axons, (chemical across synapses)	Information passes as a chemical substance through blood stream
2 Rapid transmission	Slow transmission
3 Response immediate	Response usually slow. e.g. growth
4 Response short-lived	Response long lasting
5 Response very exact	Response usually widespread

The above differences are often tested as follows:

In what ways do nervous and hormonal responses differ? [8]   (LOND)

Similarly, differences between plant and animal responses often appear in exam questions, e.g.

List three ways in which the responses of mammals differ from those of flowering plants.   (LOND)

Table 7.3 Differences between plant and animal responses

Plants	Animals
1 Lack a nervous system	Possess a nervous system
2 Coordination by hormones only	Coordination by nerves and hormones
3 A prolonged stimulus usually required	A short stimulus usually required
4 Responses usually slow	Responses usually rapid
5 Response usually involve growth	Responses usually involve movement
6 Effect usually permanent	Effect usually temporary

Behaviour

This describes the variety of ways animals respond to stimuli. In lower animals, e.g. earthworms, woodlouse, behaviour is usually predictable, whilst in mammals, particularly man, responses may be extremely variable. In all cases the central nervous system controls the response. There are three simple forms of behavioural response.

1 **Taxis** (tactic movement) is the movement of the whole organism in response to a directional stimulus. Tactic movements may be towards the stimulus (positive) or away from the stimulus (negative).

Phototaxis is the response to light, **chemotaxis** the response to chemicals and **hydrotaxis** the response to water.

e.g. *Euglena* moves towards light – positive phototaxis.
   Woodlice move away from light – negative phototaxis.
   Sperm swim towards substances produced by the egg – positive chemotaxis.
   Mosquitoes avoid insect repellent – negative chemotaxis.

2 **Kinesis** (kinetic movement) is a response shown by an organism where the rate of movement is related to the intensity of stimulation and not the direction, e.g. the waving of tentacles in *Hydra* increases with the addition of food substances to the water.

Taxes and kineses can be demonstrated on small invertebrates by the use of a choice-chamber.

Experiment *To investigate the response of woodlice to a choice of damp and dry environments.*

Apparatus

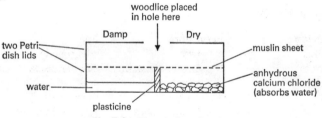

Fig. 7.21 The choice-chamber

Method The apparatus was set up as in Fig. 7.21 and ten woodlice were placed in the centre of the upper dish. The atmosphere in one half of the chamber was kept drier than the other half by the use of anhydrous calcium chloride. All other factors, e.g. light and temperature, were kept constant. Recordings were taken of the activity of the woodlice every 2 minutes for 20 minutes.

Results Typical data reveal that for most of the time the woodlice on the dry side were moving whereas those on the damp side were stationary. After 20 minutes most of the woodlice were found on the damp side and stationary.

Conclusions Woodlice respond to a dry atmosphere by increased movement – this is a kinetic response. Woodlice move towards and tend to settle in a damp atmosphere in preference to a dry atmosphere – this is a positive hydrotactic response.

Check that this topic is on your syllabus before revising it.

Describe with experimental detail, how you could demonstrate one tactic response. [8]   (O & C)

Questions of the type given could include the detail given in the experiment.

3 **Reflex** is an immediate and specific response to a stimulus and involves a reflex arc (*see* p126).

Higher animals, e.g. birds, show complex behaviour patterns such as courtship, nest-building and migration. This is **instinctive behaviour**. Mammals show remarkable abilities of being able to store information from past experience and use this to calculate the best response for the situation. This is called **learning** and is an ability associated with intelligence.

Key words

irritability	nerve fibre	iris
stimulus	synapse	ciliary body
receptors	transmitter substance	ciliary muscle
impulse	reflex arc	lens
effector	reflex action	fovea
response	conditioned reflex	aqueous humour
coordination	learning	vitreous humour
homeostatic	brain	blind spot
hormones	cerebrum	optic nerve
tropism	cerebral cortex	pupil
phototropism	association centres	suspensory ligament
geotropism	exteroceptor	accommodation
auxins	interoceptor	short sight
clinostat	proprioceptor	long sight
CNS	eye	rods
neurone	eyelid	cones
sensory neurone	conjunctiva	colour vision
intermediate neurone	cornea	stereo vision
motor neurone	sclerotic	compound eye
nerve	choroid	ommatidium

ear
pinna
Eustachian tube
ossicles
oval window
perilymph
cochlea
organ of Corti
auditory nerve
utriculus
sacculus
otoliths
ampulla
cupula
endolymph
muscles
glands
exocrine
endocrine
pituitary
thyroid
pancreas
adrenals
reproductive glands
feed-back
behaviour
taxis
phototaxis
chemotaxis
hydrotaxis
kinesis

Past examination questions

1 *Irritability in a plant and in a mammal is shown in the following two examples. Germinated maize grains, with coleoptiles 1 cm long, were illuminated from one side only. The effect on a grain, after 24 hours, is shown in A.*

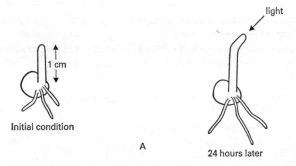

A

Light entering a human eye was changed from dim to bright. The effect, after 2 seconds, is shown in B.

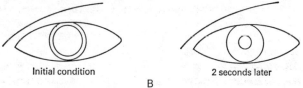

B

(a) In A what was
   (i) the stimulus, (ii) the receptor region, (iii) the effector region, (iv) the response?
(b) How was the response made by the effector in A?
(c) In B what was
   (i) the stimulus, (ii) the receptor tissue, (iii) the effector tissue, (iv) the response?
(d) How was the response made by the effector in B?
(e) (i) Describe an experiment to show which part of the coleoptile was the receptor. (Use information given on p122).
   (ii) Describe an experiment to show which part of the coleoptile was the effector. (Use information given on p122)
(f) A shows a tropism.
   (i) What is a tropism?
   (ii) Briefly describe one other example of a tropism.
(g) B shows a reflex action.
   (i) What is a reflex action?
   (ii) Briefly describe one other reflex action.
   (iii) What is a conditioned reflex action?
   (iv) Briefly describe one example of a conditioned reflex action.
(h) State **three** ways in which tropisms in plants differ from reflex actions in animals.
(i) In B the human eye was affected by the intensity of light. Briefly describe one way in which a flowering plant may be affected by the intensity of light. (AEB)

2 (a) What is the biological meaning of the term sensitivity (irritability)?
 (b) Give an example of sensitivity in
   (i) a **named** invertebrate, e.g. an earthworm,
   (ii) the root of a flowering plant.
 (c) How do plants respond to the external stimulus of light?
 (d) How may the smell of appetizing food cause a person's mouth to water? (CAM)

3 Which one of the following parts of the brain is relatively larger in man than in other animals?
 A cerebrum
 B medulla
 C cerebellum
 D hypothalamus. (CAM)

4 Which one of the following prevents the internal reflection of light in the mammalian eye?
   A cornea
   B sclerotic
   C choroid
   D conjunctiva. (CAM)
5 Explain the functioning of the following parts of the mammalian ear: (a) pinna (external ear flap), (b) semicircular canals, (c) Eustachian tube. (CAM)

Questions 6–10 are concerned with the following terms associated with the mammalian nervous system and behaviour:

A Stimulus
B Receptor
C Impulse
D Synapse
E Effector.

Relate each of the descriptions below with one of the terms above.
   6 A hammer which strikes the knee below the patella.
   7 An electrical disturbance which passes along a nerve fibre.
   8 A cell in the cochlea which sends messages to the brain when a jet aeroplane flies overhead.
   9 The triceps muscle, which contracts when a hot plate is dropped.
  10 The gap which occurs between one neurone and the next. (LOND)

8 Skeleton and locomotion

Movement Change in position of one structure relative to another.
Locomotion Movement of an organism from one place to another.
Endoskeleton A skeleton inside an organism.
Exoskeleton A skeleton outside the body of an organism.
Vertebrate An animal possessing a vertebral column.
Voluntary muscle A muscle under the conscious control of the brain.
Contraction Shortening and thickening of muscle fibres.

Skeletons

All **skeletons** are resistant to compression, and provide a rigid framework for the body. They perform the functions of

1 *support* – involves raising the body off the ground to allow efficient movement, suspension of soft parts of the body, maintenance of body shape;
2 *protection* – of internal organs; and
3 *movement* – provide attachment for muscles, and form levers on which muscles can act.

Three types of skeleton are evident in the animal kingdom.

1 Hydrostatic (in soft bodied animals, e.g. earthworm)
Fluid is secreted within the body, and presses against the body muscles. In turn the muscles are able to contract against the fluid. The combined effect of fluid pressure and muscle contraction maintains the shape and form of the animal.

2 Exoskeleton (in arthropods)
This is a hard outer covering called the cuticle, and is composed of

chitin. At the joints it is soft and flexible. Limbs are jointed and hollow and possess inward extensions for muscle attachment.

3 Endoskeleton (in vertebrates)
It is composed of cartilage or **bone**. Bone consists of inorganic calcium phosphate, organic protein, bone cells and blood vessels. Limbs are jointed, and bones are internal to muscles.

Mammal skeleton (e.g. man)
Consists of many bones of various shapes, held together by **ligaments** to form joints. It may be subdivided into two parts:

1 Axial skeleton (skull, vertebral column, ribs and sternum)
The **skull** consists of a thick cranium which protects the brain; cavities to house the eyes, ears and olfactory organs; jaws (and attached muscles) for mastication and speaking.

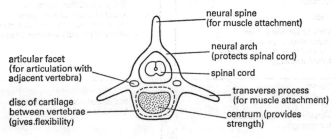

Fig. 8.1 Structure of a vertebra

The **vertebral column** consists of many **vertebrae**, placed upon each other to form a flexible rod, the backbone. Each vertebra has the typical plan shown in Fig. 8.1. Vertebrae perform three main functions:

1 protect spinal cord,
2 permit flexible movement of the body,
3 determine the posture of the body.

All vertebrae have the same basic structure, but show slight differences individually in different regions (*see* question 1, p155).

The **ribs** and **sternum**, together with the thoracic vertebrae, form the walls of the thoracic cavity which contain and protect the heart and lungs. Intercostal muscles are attached to the ribs enabling the volume of the thoracic cavity to be changed during ventilation movements.

Skeleton and locomotion 147

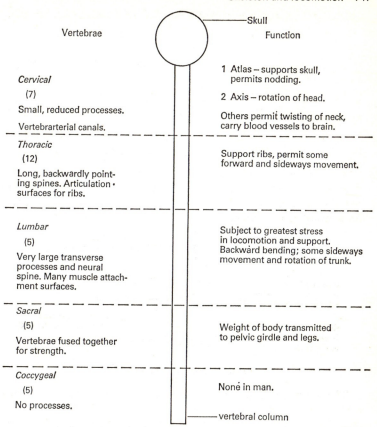

Fig. 8.2 Variation in vertebra structure and function

2 Appendicular skeleton (girdles and limbs)

Pectoral girdle is attached to vertebral column by tendons and muscles; allows great mobility of forelimbs; can act as a shock absorber (e.g. frog).

Pelvic girdle is firmly connected to vertebral column; transmits backward thrust of hind limbs against the ground to the body.

Limbs – the skeletal arrangement of both fore and hind limbs is based on the pentadactyl limb design. This is common to all land vertebrates.

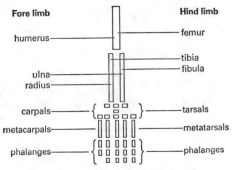

Fig. 8.3 Pentadactyl limb

Vertebrate joints

Joints are formed wherever bones meet. There are three main types of joint:

1 **immovable**, e.g. in skull and pelvis;
2 slightly movable (**cartilaginous**), e.g. vertebral column;
3 movable (**synovial**), e.g. elbow and hip.

The main types of synovial joint are:

(a) ball and socket – enables movement in all planes (hip and shoulder),
(b) hinge – movement in one plane only (knee and elbow),
(c) gliding – two surfaces slide over each other (wrist, ankle joints).

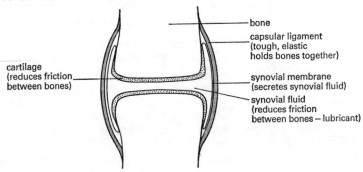

Fig. 8.4 Structure of a synovial joint

By means of a large labelled diagram, describe the structure of a movable joint in the mammalian skeleton. [5]   (O & C)

Muscle tissue

This is made up of elongated fibres which have the ability to contract and relax. A **muscle**, e.g. biceps, is a collection of muscle fibres. When a muscle contracts it shortens and thickens. This brings its two ends closer together. It may shorten to two thirds of its original length and relax back to its original length.

Muscles are well supplied with blood which brings the food and oxygen required to produce energy for the work they perform (contraction). The blood flow can be adjusted according to muscle need.

Each muscle has its own nerve supply consisting of

1 **motor neurones** which activate (stimulate) the muscle fibres to contract,
2 **sensory neurones** (from proprioceptors) which indicate the relative position of the muscle.

Muscle contraction occurs as shown in Fig. 8.5.

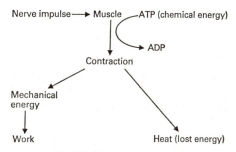

Fig. 8.5 Muscle contraction

Muscle attached to bone is called skeletal, striated or voluntary muscle. Muscles are attached to bone by tendons which are inelastic and able to withstand sudden stress. Each muscle possesses at least two points of attachment to bone:

1 origin – to a firm, fixed part of the skeleton,
2 insertion – to a mobile part of the skeleton.

Skeletal muscles usually act in pairs, the two muscles of a pair having an opposing action. When one of the pair contracts, the other must relax for movement to take place. These pairs are called **antagonistic muscles**, and are classified according to the type of movement they produce in the limbs.

Flexors bend a limb at a joint.
Extensors straighten a limb at a joint.
Abductors move a limb away from the body.
Adductors move a limb towards the body.

Some muscles work together to rotate a limb or other part of the body to produce precise movement.

Movement is produced by the contraction and relaxation of antagonistic muscles which are attached to bones acting as levers. The joint acts as the fulcrum (*see* Figs 8.6, 8.7).

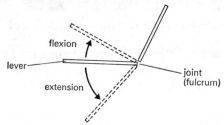

Fig. 8.6 Movement at a joint

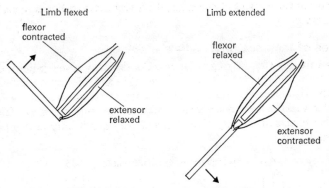

Fig. 8.7 Movement at the elbow joint

With the aid of a diagram show how a pair of antagonistic muscles brings about movement in a mammalian limb. [5]   (JMB)

Arthropod joints

Antagonistic muscles are encased within the exoskeleton, and attached to inwardly projecting processes. The joints of arthropods (Fig. 8.8) operate on the same mechanical principles as endoskeletal joints.

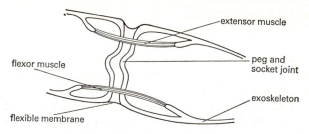

Fig. 8.8 Arthropod peg and socket joint

Using the information given above answer the following question.

In what way is the relationship between the muscles and the skeleton in this insect leg different from the relationships between muscles and the skeleton of the human arm? (AEB)

Locomotion

This occurs as a result of coordinated activity between bones, muscles and nerves.

Types of locomotion in selected animals

1 Swimming (e.g. herring) The shape of the body is streamlined, the only projections being the fins. These are thin and offer little resistance to forward movement. Most fish with bony skeletons possess a swim bladder. Gas (mainly oxygen) may be secreted into it or withdrawn from it. This adjusts the density of the fish and enables it to alter its depth in the water.

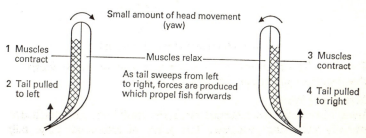

Fig. 8.9 Propulsion in fish

Forward propulsion is caused by the side-to-side movement of the broad **caudal** (tail) fin. Movement of the tail is achieved by alternate contractions of the muscles on either side of the vertebral column. The vertebral column forms a flexible rod against which the muscles of the body can pull.

The force exerted by the tail fin on the water depends on its

1 size and shape,
2 angle in the water, and
3 speed through the water.

The other vertical **fins** provide stability along the longitudinal axis of the fish and prevent **rolling** and **yawing**. The paired pectoral and pelvic fins control the amount of **pitching**. If the fish accidentally yaws, pitches or rolls, the corrective action taken by the fins is automatic.

Describe three ways in which a named vertebrate is adapted for propulsion through water. [3]   (JMB)

2 Crawling (e.g. frog)   Those limbs of the frog which are diagonally opposite each other push against the ground at the same time, e.g. right front limb with left hind limb, and left front limb with right hind limb.

3 Leaping (e.g. frog)   The hind limbs are long and folded beneath the body. When a jump is made, each joint of the hind limbs is straightened by contraction of the powerful hind limb extensor muscles. The thrust of such an action is transmitted along the limb bones to the vertebral column via the pelvic girdle. The extremely long bones of the hind limbs act as levers and increase the efficiency of jumping. Part of the energy required for the jump is used for upward movement and part for forward movement. On landing, the short forelimbs and flexible pectoral girdle soften the shock of landing.

4 Walking (e.g. dog)   The forward thrust is generated by alternate contractions of the extensor and flexor muscles of the hindlegs. These connect the pelvic girdle to the femurs of the legs. When the extensor muscles contract the hind limbs move backwards. The feet then press against the ground, and an equal and opposite force is transmitted through the body. This lifts the body clear of the ground and produces forward motion. Only one leg is raised at a time, the other three forming a tripod over which the body is balanced.

Explain the action of the muscles on the bones which are involved in walking two steps. [11]   (O & C)

Skeleton and locomotion 153

5 Running (e.g. dog) The forelimbs move forward together, followed by the hind limbs. There is now no three point suspension of the limbs. Each limb is in contact with the ground for less time than in walking. The speed of the animal is further increased when the back muscles contract. This arches the backbone and serves to increase the power of the limbs.

6 Flapping flight (e.g. pigeon) Birds wings act as **aerofoils**. Increased pressure beneath the wing provides vertical lift (*see* Fig. 8.10). When the pectoralis major muscles contract (Fig. 8.11) the wings are pulled downwards and forwards. This gives lift and some forward thrust.

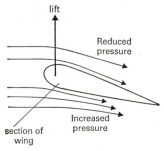

Fig. 8.10 Aerofoil effect of wings

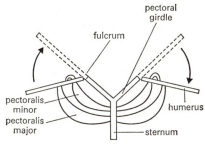

Fig. 8.11 Section of bird skeleton to show how muscles and bones operate together

Contraction of the antagonistic pectoralis minor muscles produces the upward and backward movement of the wings. This action provides *most* of the forward thrust.

Briefly explain how forward movement is achieved by the action of the bird's wing. [4] (JMB)

Steering in the air is controlled by the tail and/or unequal strikes (beats) of the wings. They also can act as brakes, especially during landing.

Adaptations of bird for flight
1. Keeled sternum for attachment of flight muscles.
2. Shortening of tail cuts down drag, increases manoeuvrability.
3. Lightening of body by hollow bones.
4. Large wing span.
5. Feathers provide smooth surface for air to pass over.
6. Fusion of bones of forelimbs.
7. Lengthening of hind limbs so that wings do not hit ground when flapping during take off.
8. High body temperature offsets cooling effect of air as bird flies through it.
9. Remarkable muscular coordination.
10. Air sacs improve ventilation.

Of what use to a bird in flight are the following:
   (i) the bones are hollow and air filled,
   (ii) the sternum (breastbone) has a large ridge or keel,
  (iii) the body is streamlined? (AEB)

Support in plants
The tissues which contribute towards the support of plants are

1. parenchyma – by turgor (*see* p31),
2. collenchyma – cell walls unevenly thickened with cellulose,
3. sclerenchyma ⎫
4. xylem   ⎭ – cell walls thickened with lignin.

For a full account of the structure and functions of these tissues *see* p20. Movement in plants is covered on p121.

Key words

skeletons
hydrostatic
exoskeleton
endoskeleton
bone
axial

skull
vertebral column
vertebrae
neural spine
neural arch
transverse process

articulating
spinal cord
centrum
cervical
thoracic
lumbar

sacral	metatarsals	biceps
coccygeal	pentadactyl	triceps
appendicular	joints	locomotion
pectoral girdle	immovable	swimming
pelvic girdle	cartilaginous	caudal
humerus	synovial	fins
radius	ligament	rolling
ulna	cartilage	yawing
carpals	muscle	pitching
metacarpals	tendons	crawling
phalanges	antagonistic	leaping
femur	flexors	walking
tibia	extensors	running
fibula	abductors	flight
tarsals	adductors	aerofoils

Past examination questions

1 *Draw and label a generalized diagram of a vertebra in either anterior (front) or posterior (rear) view. Explain the function of the vertebra in relation to (a) support, (b) the central nervous system and spinal nerves, (c) muscles and movement.* (CAM)
(*See* p146 *for diagram.*)

2 *Complete the following sentences.*
  (a) *The elbow is an example of a . . ., whereas the shoulder is an example of a . . .*
  (b) *The spinal cord runs through a series of bones called . . . Those in the neck region are called . . .*
  (c) *A muscle is attached to a bone by means of a . . ., whereas two bones are joined together by . . .*
  (d) *Muscles of the limb bones work in pairs: the one that straightens the limb is called the . . . and the one that bends the limb is called the . . . Pairs of muscles that work in this way are called . . .* (CAM)

3 *In which order do the regions of the vertebral column of a mammal occur?*
  A sacral – thoracic – cervical – lumbar
  B lumbar – thoracic – cervical – sacral
  C thoracic – cervical – sacral – lumbar
  D cervical – thoracic – lumbar – sacral. (CAM)

4 (a) *State two functions of the vertebral column, other than its function of allowing movement.* [1, 1]

(b) Give a reason why: (i) the largest mammals are found in the sea; (ii) the legs of a rhinoceros are shorter and thicker than those of a horse. [1, 1]

(c) State two ways in which the structure of a water plant stem differs from that of a land plant. [1, 1] (SCE)

5 Draw a detailed diagram showing the muscles and skeleton of a mammalian limb joint. Explain the functions of the following in bringing about movement of the limb: (a) opposing muscles, (b) bones, (c) tendons, (d) the joint. [25] (LOND)

6 The diagrams below show three positions of a toad as it 'takes off' into a jump.

What part is played in 'take off' by the (a) extensor muscles of the hind limb, (b) flexor muscles of the hind limb, (c) skeleton of the hind limb, (d) joints of the hind limb, (e) firm ground below the feet? (AEB)

9 Reproduction, growth and development

Reproduction The production of a new generation of individuals of the same species.

Gamete A specialized haploid cell produced for sexual reproduction.

Haploid A single set of chromosomes (n) consisting of one chromosome from each pair of homologous chromosomes.

Fertilization The fusion of the haploid nucleus of the male gamete with the haploid nucleus of the female gamete to form a diploid zygote.

Zygote The diploid product of fusion of two gametes.

Diploid The number of chromosomes (2n) found in body cells, made up of homologous pairs.

Spore An asexually produced body, produced in large numbers which may develop directly into a new organism.

Zygospore A zygote formed by the fusion of two similar gametes and possessing a thick protective wall which is able to resist adverse conditions.

Perennation The method of survival of some plants from year to year by vegetative means.

Pollination The transfer of pollen from the ripe anther of one flower to the stigma of the same flower, or a different flower of the same species.

Seed A ripened fertilized ovule, containing an embryo which may grow into a new plant.

Fruit The ripened ovary of a flower containing seeds.

Germination The development of a seed into a photosynthesizing plant.

Hermaphrodite An organism possessing functional male and female gonads.

Growth An irreversible increase in the amount of protoplasm in an organism.

Metamorphosis A change in body form during the life cycle.

Reproduction

Reproduction is a characteristic of living organisms. There are two forms of reproduction, **asexual** and **sexual**.

Main features of asexual reproduction
1 Offspring formed from one parent.
2 All offspring are genetically identical to each other and their parent – no variation.
3 Rapid multiplication in numbers in favourable conditions.

Asexual reproduction occurs by a type of cell division called **mitosis** in which

1 exact duplication of genetic material (chromosomes) occurs within the nucleus of the parent cell;
2 the nucleus divides and each daughter nucleus receives identical genetic material;
3 cytoplasm divides to produce two daughter cells.

Mitosis is a component of growth in all multicellular organisms and a means of producing a new generation in a variety of simpler organisms.

Some of the most common methods of asexual reproduction are:

1 Binary fission Division of an acellular organism into two identical individuals which then separate, e.g. *Amoeba*, bacteria.

2 Fragmentation An organism may be broken into two or more pieces which can continue to live independently, e.g. *Spirogyra*.

3 Spores Cells divide by mitosis to produce spores which are dispersed. Each spore is capable of developing into a new individual, e.g. *Mucor*.

4 Budding Rapid cell division leads to an outgrowth (bud) on the body of the parent. This separates and becomes independent, e.g. *Hydra*.

5 Vegetative propagation A feature of some flowering plants, it involves the separation of a well-differentiated structure from its parent. This structure then develops into a new plant.

6 Artificial propagation Horticulturalists use this method to maintain desirable characters in their stock, e.g. cuttings – short shoot lengths, bearing leaves are planted in moist compost. They quickly develop adventitious roots and grow into new plants (e.g. geranium).

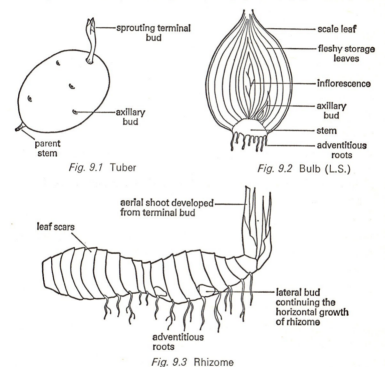

Fig. 9.1 Tuber

Fig. 9.2 Bulb (L.S.)

Fig. 9.3 Rhizome

Advantages of vegetative propagation (reproduction)
1 Offspring are genetically identical, therefore able to survive in conditions which are favourable to parents.
2 Can withstand unfavourable conditions using stored food.
3 Localized spreading may prevent competition from other species.
4 It is the only way that specialized varieties can be grown (propagated) without change.

Disadvantages of vegetative propagation
1 Overcrowding may occur.
2 New varieties can not be produced vegetatively.
3 Disease may spread rapidly, since being genetically alike they may all be affected by the same disease.

Table 9.1 Some examples of organs of vegetative propagation

Organ	Description	Example
Stem tuber (Fig. 9.1)	A swollen end of an underground lateral stem.	Potato
Bulb (Fig. 9.2)	A small, vertically growing underground stem, surrounded by fleshy leaves containing food reserves.	Onion
Rhizome (Fig. 9.3)	An underground, horizontally growing stem, swollen with food reserves.	Iris

Perennation
Some organs of vegetative propagation are also organs of **perennation**. There are two types of perennial plants.

1 *Herbaceous perennials*. Aerial parts die down. Underground parts persist containing food stores which are utilized for rapid growth in the following spring, e.g. *Iris* (rhizome), daffodil (bulb).

2 *Woody perennials*. Aerial parts persist bearing buds. These are supplied with food stored in the stems and roots. They develop in spring into new branches, e.g. oak (deciduous perennial), holly (evergreen perennial).

(a) *Make a fully labelled diagram of the organ of perennation of a named flowering plant.* [5]
(b) *Give two advantages of perennation and two advantages of variability among offspring.* [4]   (o)

Main features of sexual reproduction
1 Involves the fusion of two **gametes** usually from two different individuals of the same species.
2 The offspring are genetically different from either parent. This produces variation within the species (*see* p193).

3 The zygote is often adapted for survival in adverse conditions, e.g. zygospore of *Mucor*.

Pick out the main features of the two forms of reproduction and answer this question:

Distinguish between asexual and sexual reproduction. (LOND)

Gamete production

The nucleus of every cell in the body of an organism contains a fixed number of chromosomes. This number is made up of pairs of homologous chromosomes.

When male and female gametes fuse to form a **zygote**, each contributes an equal number of chromosomes. Therefore each gamete contains only half the number of chromosomes of the zygote (**haploid number**, or '**n**').

Haploid gametes are produced by a special type of cell division called **meiosis** (reduction division) shown in Fig. 9.4

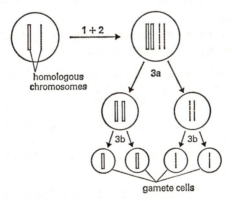

Fig. 9.4 Meiosis

The main points of meiosis are:

1 Exact duplication of genetic material.
2 Pairing of homologous chromosomes.
3 Halving of chromosome content to produce haploid condition by separation of homologous chromosomes, so that one chromosome from each pair goes into each gamete.

Fertilization

Fusion of male and female gametes restores the **diploid** chromosome number and produces the zygote (Fig. 9.5). The zygote contains

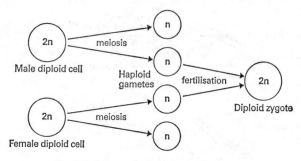

Fig. 9.5 Gamete formation and fertilization

hereditary material which is different from that of either parent, and this difference is a source of variety in that species.

Sexual reproduction in selected organisms

In *Spirogyra*, adjacent filaments **conjugate**. The entire cellular contents of one filament pass through conjugation tubes into the other – fertilization occurs and **zygospores** are produced. The original cells disappear following sexual reproduction.

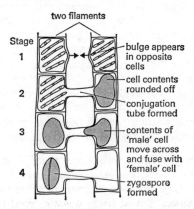

Fig. 9.6 Reproduction in *Spirogyra*

Reproduction, growth and development 163

In *Mucor*, parts of the hyphae of opposite mating strains swell to form **gametangia**. They meet, and their walls break down. Fusion of nuclear material takes place and a zygospore is produced.

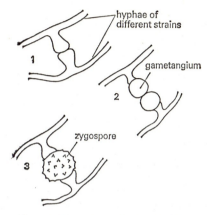

Fig. 9.7 Sexual reproduction in *Mucor*

In multicellular organisms which display division of labour, specific parts of the body, called gonads, produce the gametes.

Hermaphrodites (e.g. *Hydra*, tapeworm, earthworm, many flowering plants) are able to produce male and female gametes within their own body. Often where this is so, mechanisms operate which prevent self fertilization, e.g. **protandry** (male gametes are formed and released before female gametes are mature) and **protogyny** (female gametes are formed and released before male gametes are mature).

In other organisms the sexes are separate and the male and female gametes are produced by individuals of different sex.

Different environmental conditions may affect the number of gametes produced, the method of fertilization and the mode of development of the embryo. External fertilization may take place in aquatic organisms, whereas on land fertilization takes place within the body of the female.

1 Fish (e.g. herring) Gametes shed into water. Chances of gametes fusing (external fertilization) low as gametes disperse in water. Shoaling, and production of large numbers of gametes offset this by increasing chances of fertilization. Young hatch quickly. Feed on plankton. No parental care.

2 Frog Pairing occurs. Male, on female's back, sheds sperms as eggs laid. External fertilization but increased chance of fertilization. Fewer gametes than fish. Egg contains yolk and protective jelly. Larval stage with gills and tail, limbs develop and gills and tail lost. **Metamorphosis** into adult. No parental care.

3 Bird (e.g. robin) Male possesses territory. Pairing in spring. Hen builds nest. Mating occurs followed by internal fertilization. Fewer eggs necessary as this method increases chances of fertilization. Clutch of about five shelled eggs produced. Yolk in eggs nourishes developing

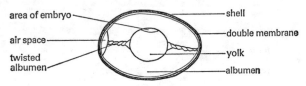

Fig. 9.8 Structure of a bird's egg

embryo (*see* Fig. 9.8). Egg incubated by hen to speed up rate of development. Fledgling fed by both parents. Becomes independent 6 weeks after hatching.

Describe egg production and parental care in a named amphibian and a named bird. [12]   (O & C)

Sexual reproduction in mammals (e.g. man)

Placental female mammals produce fewer ova than fish and birds since their higher success rate of fertilization, their method of protection and nourishment provided during development, birth at an advanced stage (viviparity) and an extended period of parental care ensure that more offspring reach maturity.

Sperm production

Spermatozoa are produced in the **seminiferous tubules** of the **testes**. The testes are held in the **scrotal sac** just outside the body cavity because sperm need a lower temperature for development. Sperms pass from the testes as follows:

tubules → epididymis → vas deferens → urethra
(produced)   (stored)   (during ejaculation)   (penis)

Reproduction, growth and development 165

Secretions from the **seminal vesicle** and **prostate gland** are added to sperm to activate them into swimming.

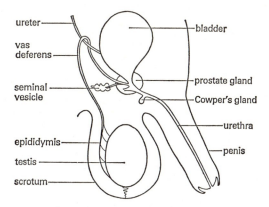

Fig. 9.9 Male reproductive organs

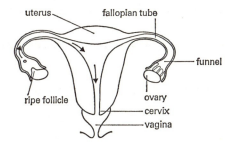

Fig. 9.10 Female reproductive organs

Egg production

Every 28 days one of the **ovaries** releases an **ovum**. It passes through the reproductive system as shown by arrows in the diagram. The development of the ovum, its release (**ovulation**) and subsequent events occur in a cyclical process controlled by hormones. This is called the **menstrual (oestrous) cycle** (*see* Fig. 9.13) and is modified if **pregnancy** occurs. Each month the **uterus** is prepared to receive the developing **embryo** in case fertilization occurs. When no embryo is present the uterus lining is shed and the ovary produces another ovum.

Table 9.2 Differences between male and female gametes in man

Sperm	Egg (ovum)
1 Are able to propel themselves	Unable to propel themselves
2 Very small (2.5 µm across widest part)	Much larger than sperms (120 µm in diameter)
3 No food reserves	Cytoplasm with yolky droplets provides a source of food for embryo during initial stages of development
4 Vast numbers expelled during each ejaculation	Usually produced singly at monthly intervals

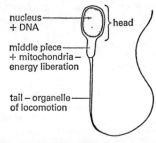

Fig. 9.11 Human sperm

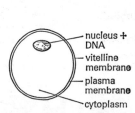

Fig. 9.12 Human ovum

Menstrual cycle

This is controlled by hormones, as described on p167.

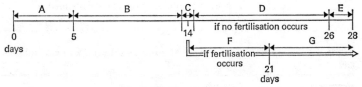

Fig. 9.13 Menstrual cycle

A Uterine lining expelled from body – menstruation.

B **Graafian follicle** in ovary develops; egg ripens and follicle produces **oestrogen**; uterus lining thickens.

C Follicle releases egg (ovulation) and develops into **corpus luteum**.

D Corpus luteum secretes **progesterone** – maintains uterus lining.

E Corpus luteum breaks down; progesterone level falls; cycle begins at A again.

If fertilization occurs
F Embryo implants in uterus wall by day 21.
G Corpus luteum persists and secretes progesterone which maintains uterus lining – no menstruation and normal cycle stops whilst embryo develops.

Table 9.3 Functions of hormones in female mammal (grouped under site of origin)

Hormone	Function
Pituitary gland	
Follicle stimulating hormone (FSH)	1 Stimulates Graafian follicle development in ovary 2 Stimulates ovary to secrete oestrogen
Luteinizing hormone (LH)	1 Causes ovulation 2 Conversion of Graafian follicle into corpus luteum 3 Stimulates secretion of progesterone
Oxytocin	1 Stimulates uterine muscle contraction in labour 2 Stimulates flow of milk
Prolactin	1 Promotes secretion of milk
Ovary	
Oestrogen	1 Causes onset and maintenance of secondary sexual characteristics, e.g. breasts develop, fat deposited, hair under arms and pubic areas, wider pelvic girdle, greater awareness of sex 2 Aids healing/repair of uterus wall after menstruation 3 Increases thickness of uterus wall
Corpus luteum	
Progesterone	1 Prepares uterine wall for implantation 2 Maintains uterus lining in early pregnancy 3 Inhibits oxytocin

Table 9.4 Functions of hormones in male mammal (grouped under site of origin)

Hormone	Function
Pituitary gland	
FSH	1 Stimulates sperm production
LH	1 Stimulates testes to secrete male hormones
Testis	
Testosterone	1 Causes onset and maintenance of male secondary sexual characteristics, e.g. muscular body, voice deepens, genitals enlarge, hair under arms, pubic area, face and chest

Copulation and fertilization

The erect **penis** is inserted into the **vagina** of the female during mating, and sperms are discharged. They swim towards the **oviduct** where fertilization may occur.

The fertilized egg begins to divide mitotically, and becomes **implanted** in the wall of the uterus. The **placenta** develops from tissue derived partly from the uterine wall and partly from that of the embryo (Fig. 9.14).

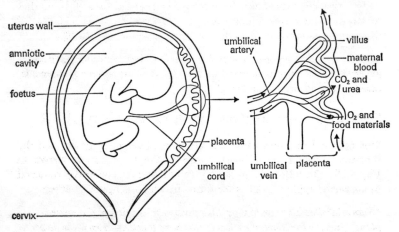

Fig. 9.14 Foetus, placenta and uterus

An **umbilical cord** connects the embryo to the placenta. The blood vessels of the placenta form an intimate association with the uterine blood vessels (*see* Fig. 9.14). No mixing of the mother's blood and foetal blood takes place. Diffusion of oxygen and dissolved food materials from mother to **foetus**, and carbon dioxide and soluble excretory products (e.g. urea) from foetus to mother takes place. The placenta also produces oestrogen and progesterone throughout pregnancy.

The foetus is contained in the **amnion** which is filled with **amniotic fluid**. This serves to protect the foetus from buffeting and sudden temperature changes, and enables the foetus to move about freely.

Briefly outline the menstrual cycle of a woman and describe what changes occur in her between fertilization of the egg and giving birth. [10] (o)

Reproduction, growth and development

Birth

Full development normally takes 280 days – the **gestation** period. Prior to normal birth the baby has its head placed downwards in the uterus. Oxytocin produces periodic gently rhythmic contractions of the uterine wall. They increase in intensity and number. The amnion bursts, liberating the amniotic fluid, and the foetus is expelled from the body. The placenta follows as 'after-birth', and the umbilical cord is tied and cut.

The offspring may **suckle** from the **mammary glands** of the mother which have been developing during pregnancy. Humans take care of their young and protect them through the early years of their life.

Describe how the embryo of a named mammal receives protection, food and oxygen during its gestation period. In what ways do the parents of mammals care for their offspring after birth? (LOND)

Sexual reproduction in a flowering plant

It is essential that you know the structure of a named flower and the functions of its parts. The structure of the buttercup is shown in Fig. 9.15. The following question is typical and the knowledge required to answer it applies to all other forms in which it might be asked.

Draw a labelled diagram to show the structure of the flower of a named plant. Give the functions of each part you have labelled. How is the flower adapted to its method of pollination? (LOND)

Pollination

Pollination must take place in flowering plants before fertilization can occur. There are two types of pollination:

1 **Self pollination** Pollen from the **anther** of a flower is transferred to the **stigma** of the same flower, or a flower on the same plant. It is prevented when the **stamens** and **carpels** (a) ripen at different times, or (b) are situated in different regions of the flower, or (c) have incompatible gametes. In some species there are separate male and female flowers and plants.

State two ways in which flowering plants may avoid self-fertilization. (CAM)

2 **Cross pollination** Pollen is transferred from the anther of one

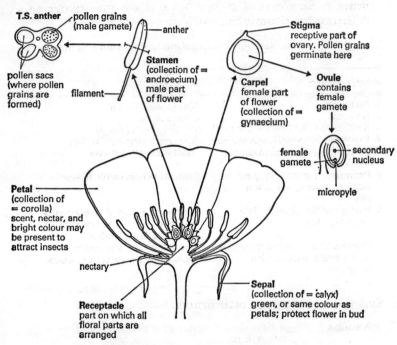

Fig. 9.15 Structure of buttercup flower

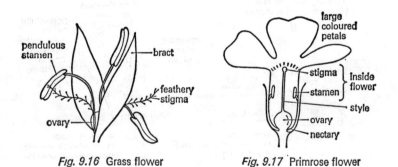

Fig. 9.16 Grass flower

Fig. 9.17 Primrose flower

flower to the stigma of another flower of the same species on a different plant. This may be aided by wind or insects.

Table 9.5 A comparison of the characteristics of wind and insect pollinated flowers

Wind pollinated	Insect pollinated
1 No nectar	May possess nectar
2 No scent	Often scented
3 Small petals, not brightly coloured	Large, coloured petals
4 Feathery stigma with large surface area to trap pollen, often hangs outside flower	Stigma sticky to hold pollen, enclosed within flower
5 Pendulous stamens, hanging outside flower to aid pollen release	Stamens remain within flower
6 Vast quantities of small, light, smooth pollen	Smaller quantities of heavy pollen which is often spiny and sticky to adhere to insect bodies
7 Flowers often open before leaves which might hinder pollen reception	Flower structure adapted to pollination by one type of insect

Events leading up to fertilization

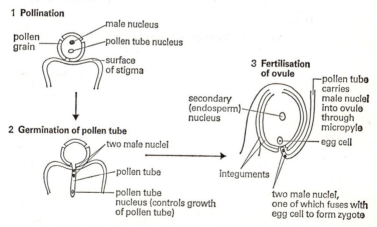

Fig. 9.18 Events leading up to fertilization

Distinguish between pollination and fertilization. (CAM)

After fertilization (e.g. broad bean)

1 The floral parts gradually wither away.
2 The zygote divides mitotically and differentiates into (a) a **radicle** (embryonic root), (b) a **plumule** (embryonic shoot), and (c) two **cotyledons**.
3 The **integuments** become the **testa** (seed coat) which is often lignified, tough and protective. At the end of this development a **seed** is formed (*see* Fig. 9.19).

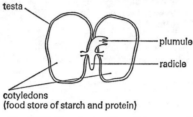

Fig. 9.19 Structure of broad bean seed

Fruit formation

The ovary containing the seed or seeds has in the meantime developed into the **fruit**. Its wall has increased in size to become the **pericarp**. The main functions of the fruit are to protect the seeds and to aid their dispersal. Fruits are variable in form and size.

Fruit and seed dispersal

As plants are generally fixed, they must employ effective methods to disperse their offspring. Dispersal allows colonization of new habitats and diminishes competition with the parent plant for space, light and water. The agencies for such dispersal are

1 wind,
2 animals,
3 self-dispersal,
4 water,
5 accidental.

Adaptations for wind dispersal The fruit or seed develops a large surface area with respect to its volume/weight. This delays the descent of the structure to the ground by offering greater resistance to the air as it falls, e.g. seed parachutes – hairy outgrowths of seed (willow herb), winged fruit – outgrowth of pericarp (sycamore).

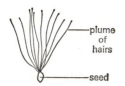

Fig. 9.20 Willowherb seed

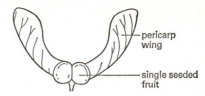

Fig. 9.21 Sycamore fruit

Adaptations for animal dispersal

1 Development of hooks/spines on fruit or seed which may catch in fur of passing animals and be carried some distance, e.g. pericarp develops hooks (goose grass).
2 Fruits may be succulent, brightly coloured and edible. (a) They may be eaten by birds. The seeds resist digestion and are egested in the bird's faeces at some distance from the parent plant. (b) The fruit may be eaten and the seeds discarded by the animal, e.g. cherry.

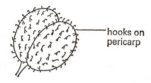

Fig. 9.22 Goose grass fruit

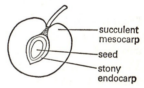

Fig. 9.23 Cherry

Adaptations for explosive self dispersal Fruit remains attached to plant, but parts of it dry unevenly. Resulting tensions burst open the fruit and the seeds are catapulted away, e.g. gorse.

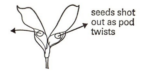

Fig. 9.24 Gorse fruit

Adaptations for water dispersal Seed or fruit may develop a fibrous layer which traps air within itself, thus allowing the structure to float, e.g. coconut.

Accidental dispersal
1 Seeds picked up with/in mud by bird's or mammal's feet.
2 Forgotten hoards of nuts and acorns gathered by squirrels.
3 Various ways of dispersal by man, e.g. farming, aeroplanes, ships.

(a) *With reference to a named example, explain how insect pollination may occur.*
(b) *With reference to a named example, explain how seed dispersal may be brought about when the seeds or fruits of a flowering plant become attached to the outside of an animal's body.* (CAM)

Table 9.6 Differences in sexual reproduction between mammals and flowering plants

Mammals	*Flowering plants*
Sexes separate	Usually hermaphrodite
Reproductive structures present throughout life	Reproductive structures temporary
Copulation; sperms swim to egg	Pollination usually by external agents; male nucleus reaches ovule via pollen tube
Offspring grows continually until maturity	Embryo often enters a dormant period as a seed before development proceeds
Offspring motile: no need for agents of dispersal	Dispersal effected by external factors
Relatively few offspring formed	Many offspring produced
Survival rate of offspring high	Survival rate low

Dormancy Dispersed seeds rarely germinate immediately, even if conditions are favourable. Seeds may be regarded as a resistant stage, able to survive conditions of cold and desiccation. This period of inactivity prior to germination is called dormancy.

Germination
External conditions necessary for dormancy to be broken and germination to begin are:

1 Water – to activate enzymes and aid hydrolysis of stored food into soluble material for transport to growing regions.
2 Optimum temperature – for optimum enzyme activity.

Reproduction, growth and development 175

3 Oxygen – for aerobic respiration to liberate the necessary energy needed for germination.

Experiment *To investigate the conditions necessary for germination.*

Method Set up four boiling tubes as shown in Fig. 9.25, with cress seeds.

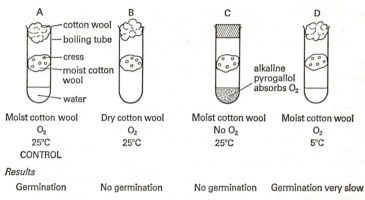

Fig. 9.25 To investigate the conditions necessary for germination

Conclusion Oxygen, an optimum temperature and water are necessary for germination.

Describe investigations which you could carry out in the laboratory to demonstrate the conditions essential for germination of seeds. [10]   (O&C)

Germination of broad bean
Water is absorbed by the bean; cotyledons swell and split testa; enzymes begin to convert insoluble food stores of cotyledons (starch/protein) into soluble components. These are passed to growing points of the plant where they are utilized.

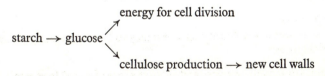

Presence of glucose also increases osmotic pressure of tissues of seed; this promotes entry of water into embryo and aids extension of newly

formed cells. Radicle grows down into soil; root hairs appear behind meristematic region. These absorb water and salts which are passed to the rest of the seedling. Lateral roots grow, anchorage provided. Plumule begins to grow upwards through soil. At surface it straightens, young leaves develop chlorophyll, photosynthesis begins.

Types of germination

1 Hypogeal Plumule is forced upwards above the ground by rapid elongation of **epicotyl**. Cotyledons remain underground and within the ruptured testa of the seed, e.g. broad bean (*see* Fig. 9.26).

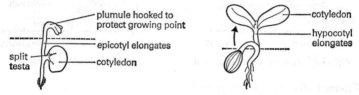

Fig. 9.26 Broad bean germination   *Fig. 9.27* Sunflower germinating

2 Epigeal Plumule and cotyledons pulled upwards above the ground by rapid elongation of the **hypocotyl**, e.g. sunflower (*see* Fig. 9.27).

Using the diagrams above as a basis, answer the following question.

Show by means of three labelled diagrams, the stages in the germination of a named seed, as far as the production of the first foliage leaf. (CAM)

Growth

Growth is a characteristic of all living organisms. Raw materials are assimilated and energy used up in order to increase the dry weight of protoplasm. Growth in multicellular organisms is accompanied by an increase in cell number.

Growth is quantitative (can be measured) and may be represented graphically. Growth in cells, tissues, organs, organisms and populations is usually measured in terms of wet weight (fresh weight), dry weight, length or number; and plotted against time. For most purposes other than population growth, dry weight (wet weight with all water removed) is more significant, particularly in plants, as it measures the exact amount of biological material present and overcomes fluid level fluctua-

Reproduction, growth and development 177

tions. Length is easy to measure but disregards growth in other directions which may be significant.

There are a variety of characteristic growth curves which show the effect of particular influences (*see* Figs 9.28, 9.29, 9.32, 9.33).

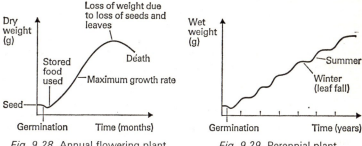

Fig. 9.28 Annual flowering plant

Fig. 9.29 Perennial plant

Factors affecting plant growth

1 **Nutrition** Carbon dioxide, water, light and mineral salts must be freely available.
2 **Auxins** Growth hormones produced at the apices of roots and shoots. Specific quantities stimulate cell division and elongation. (*see* p122)
3 **Light** Slows growth by inactivating/destroying auxins. Result of growth in complete darkness is an etiolated shoot.
4 **Temperature** If all other conditions are constant, the rate of growth varies, within certain limits, according to the temperature. Maximum metabolic activity occurs at the optimum temperature.
5 **Genetic factors** Provide potential for growth if all other factors optimal.

Growth in flowering plants Cell division is restricted to meristematic regions in the tips of roots and stems (**apical meristems**) which

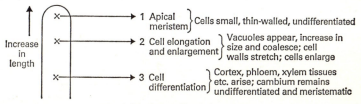

Fig. 9.30 Generalized shoot apex

provide increase in length (*see* Fig. 9.30). Cell division in the **cambium** allows increase in girth.

Increase in girth in trees This is necessary to enable the weight of branches and leaves to be supported. Increased growth requires extra

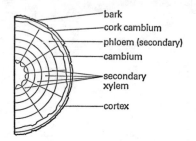

Fig. 9.31 Increase in girth of a tree

conducting tissues xylem and phloem. A continuous ring of meristematic cells (the cambium) around the stem produces extra xylem on its inside and phloem on its outside as shown in Fig. 9.31. The additional xylem forms growth rings, each of which corresponds to a year's growth. A cork cambium below the epidermis gives rise to a layer of cork which is impermeable to water.

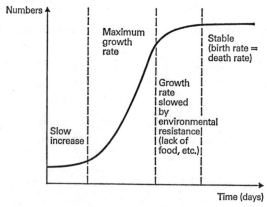

Fig. 9.32 Population growth curve (water fleas in a pond)

Growth in Arthropods

Visible growth is intermittent as a result of their hard exoskeleton. Size remains constant until **ecdysis** (formation of a new cuticle) occurs and the old exoskeleton is shed (**moulting**). Rapid increase in size follows this. Each stage between moults is called an **instar**. The adult is called an **imago**.

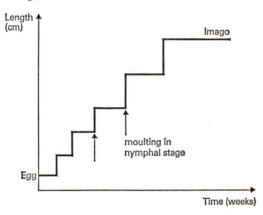

Fig. 9.33 Locust (egg–adult)

1 *Explain the following terms as used in describing insect development: (i) ecdysis; (ii) metamorphosis; (iii) nymph; (iv) imago.* [8] (O & C)
2 *Why does an insect larva periodically shed its skeleton?* [1] (JMB)

Metamorphosis Arthropods and amphibia possess larval stages in the life-cycle between egg and adult. Larvae may: 1 act as a dispersal phase; 2 act as a dormant stage during adverse conditions; 3 show

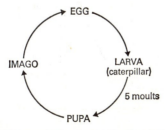

Fig. 9.34 Complete metamorphosis: the butterfly

180 Biology

adaptations to a different environment to the adult and allow time for transition to it (e.g. tadpole and frog); 4 have different habitat, feeding habits, locomotion and behaviour from adults, thus preventing competition for food and space.

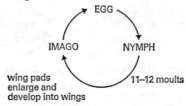

Fig. 9.35 Incomplete metamorphosis: the cockroach. Growth is accompanied by a series of gradual changes where the young nymphs look like miniature adults.

Using the information given above and your own notes and textbook answer the following question.

1 *What do you understand by the term growth as applied to living organisms?* [5]
2 *Describe, using labelled diagrams, how the life-cycle of a locust or cockroach differs from that of a butterfly or housefly.* [15] (O & C)

Growth in mammals
Growth is independent of temperature and limited since it ceases once adult size has been reached. It occurs throughout the body, but different parts of the body grow at different rates, and at different times during the growth period.

State one way in which the growth of a plant differs from that of an animal. [2] (JMB)

Key words

reproduction	budding	gametes
asexual	vegetative propagation	zygote
sexual	artificial propagation	haploid
mitosis	rhizome	meiosis
binary fission	bulb	fertilization
fragmentation	tuber	fusion
spores	perennation	diploid

Reproduction, growth and development

conjugate
zygospores
gametangia
hermaphrodite
protandry
protogyny
metamorphosis
spermatozoa
seminiferous tubules
testes
scrotal sac
epididymis
vas deferens
ejaculation
urethra
seminal vesicle
prostate gland
ovaries
ovum
ovulation
menstrual cycle
pregnancy
uterus
embryo
Graafian follicle
oestrogen
corpus luteum

progesterone
pituitary gland
FSH
LH
oxytocin
prolactin
oestrogen
testosterone
copulation
penis
vagina
oviduct
implanted
placenta
umbilical cord
foetus
amnion
amniotic fluid
gestation
suckle
mammary glands
pollination
self-pollination
anther
stigma
stamens
carpels

cross pollination
radicle
plumule
cotyledons
integuments
testa
seed
fruit
pericarp
dormancy
germination
hypogeal
epicotyl
epigeal
hypocotyl
growth
apical meristem
cambium
cell elongation
differentiation
ecdysis
moulting
instar
imago
nymph
larva

Past examination questions

1 (a) *Cells within the testis divide to form sperm cells (spermatozoa). Before this division each cell contains 23 pairs of chromosomes. A sperm cell contains 23 single chromosomes, one from each pair.*
  (i) *What term is used to describe this type of cell division?* [1]
  (ii) *How does this type of cell division produce sperm cells containing different genetic material?* [1]
  (iii) *What structural changes occur when a sperm cell is formed?* [2]
  (iv) *What determines the sex of an embryo?* [3]
  (b) *The testis also produces the hormone testosterone.*
  (i) *When is this hormone produced?* [2]

(ii) Briefly describe four effects of this hormone. [4]
(iii) How does this hormone pass to other organs? [2] (AEB)

2 The graph shows the average dry mass of whole plants of a species of an annual flowering plant plotted against time from the beginning of germination until death.

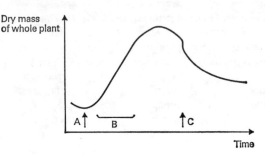

(a) Why does the mass fall to A? [2]
(b) Why does the mass rise during B? [2]
(c) Why does the mass fall sharply at C? [2]
(d) Why does the mass fall steadily after C? [2]
(e) Briefly describe, with necessary experimental detail, how you would obtain the figures necessary to plot the graph illustrated above. [5] (O)

3 (a) Complete the following table showing aspects of reproduction in various animals (cod has been filled in for you as an example).

	Number of eggs or young produced at a time	Type of fertilization	Where development takes place
cod	3–7 million	external	water
frog	1000–2000		
blackbird	3–6		in protective egg shell
wild cat	4			[3]

(b) Give one reason why the cod must produce large numbers of eggs in order for this kind of fish to survive. [1]
(c) Give one reason why the offspring of the cat have a high survival rate after birth. [1] (SCE)

4 *Describe reproduction in a named female mammal. In your answer refer to sexual cycles, mating, nutrition of the embryo, birth and maternal care. (Diagrams of the female reproductive system are not required.)*
[25] (LOND)

5 *State two ways in which the wheat flower is adapted for wind pollination.*
[2]
Tubers, produced by a potato plant, can be described as forming a clone. What is a clone? [1]
What method of reproduction produces spores? [1]
List three requirements for spore germination. [3] (SCE) (*See* p185.)

10 Genetics and evolution

F₁ generation Offspring from a first cross between individuals.
F₂ generation Offspring from a cross between F₁ progeny.
Recessive A gene which, in the presence of its contrasting allele in the heterozygote, is not expressed in the phenotype.
Dominant The gene whose characteristic appears in the heterozygous phenotype.
Chromosome A thread-like structure in the nucleus, visible at cell division.
DNA A nucleic acid whose molecular form determines hereditary characteristics.
Gene The structures in the chromosome which determine hereditary characteristics.
Homologous Corresponding chromosomes inherited from male and female parents.
Alleles Alternative forms of a gene, occupying the same place on a chromosome and affecting the same character but in different ways.
Diploid The number of chromosomes (2n) found in body cells, made up of homologous pairs.
Haploid A single set of chromosomes (n) consisting of one chromosome from each pair of homologous chromosomes.
Homozygous The condition where a pair of identical alleles occurs in the same cell.
Heterozygous The condition where a pair of contrasting alleles occur in the same cell.
Genotype The genetic composition of an organism.
Phenotype The visible physical characteristic of an organism.
Linkage The effect of genes being on the same chromosome.
Sex linkage The linkage of genes that are located on the sex chromosomes.

Genetics and evolution 185

Carrier An apparently normal heterozygote which 'carries' a recessive abnormal gene.

Heredity The passing on of characteristics through successive generations.

Mutation A sudden (abrupt) structural change in a chromosome or gene which is inheritable.

Clone A population of cells or individuals with identical genotypes derived from a single cell by mitosis.

Species The smallest unit of classification. Only organisms of the same species can interbreed and produce fertile offspring.

Natural selection The environmental selection of individuals best adapted to live and reproduce in that environment.

Genetics

The science of genetics explains how similarities and differences in characteristics arise and are inherited.

Mendelian genetics

Current theories are still based on the experimental work first performed by Gregor **Mendel**, an Austrian monk. He worked with garden peas which possess specific **characters** such as tall and dwarf plants, yellow and green cotyledons, etc.

Mendel observed each character individually and noted that a **pure breeding** tall plant always produced tall offspring, and a pure breeding dwarf plant always produced dwarf offspring. He crossed a pure tall and pure dwarf plant, collected the seeds and grew them (F_1 generation). They were all tall. He then allowed the F_1 plants to self fertilize, and collected and grew the F_2 seeds. The F_2 consisted of tall and dwarf plants in the ratio of 3 tall : 1 dwarf. Mendel concluded:

1 Offspring must possess two factors for each character.
2 Factors must be transmitted from parent to offspring via gametes.
3 For any pair of factors, only one is present in a single gamete.
4 Each factor transmitted from parent to offspring remains intact. (This is the only way that the reappearance of a recessive character can be explained.)
5 The F_1 generation, although tall, must also have received a factor for dwarfness. This factor is masked and called **recessive**. The factor for tallness is called **dominant**.

From this Mendel formulated his **'Law of Segregation of Factors'** which states:

'An organism's characters are determined by internal factors which occur in pairs. Only one of a pair of such factors can be represented in a single gamete.'

When meiosis was discovered it was recognized that the chromosome number was halved during gamete formation. This explains why only one factor is found in a single gamete.

T. H. Morgan (1866-1945) with his work on *Drosophila* established a sound basis for explaining the fundamental patterns of inheritance. He confirmed and augmented Mendel's ideas and enabled a chromosome theory of heredity to be established.

The nucleus
The nucleus has two roles.

1 It carries instructions for the daily control of the cell's activities.
2 It ensures the accurate transmission of these instructions to the daughter cells produced during mitosis and, in gamete cell production, meiosis.

Chromosomes inside the nucleus carry the instructions for all the cell's activities. Each chromosome contains a long molecule of **deoxyribonucleic acid** (DNA) covered by a protein coat. DNA is made up

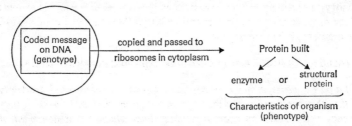

Fig. 10.1 Protein synthesis

of repeated units containing a nitrogenous base. The sequence of these bases forms a coded instruction for the production of protein molecules by protein synthesis. Most of the proteins produced directly act as enzymes allowing reactions to occur (cell metabolism). This process is summarized in Fig. 10.1.

Genetics and evolution 187

A **gene** is a region of the chromosome where the sequence of bases in the DNA carries the code for a specific protein molecule. Each chromosome is made up of very many genes arranged in linear order along the chromosome length, as shown in Fig. 10.2.

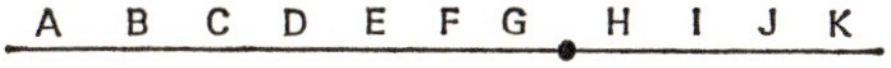

```
A  B  C  D  E  F  G  H  I  J  K
───────────────────●───────────
```

Fig. 10.2 Position of genes on chromosome

Homologous chromosomes carry genes for the same characteristics arranged in the same order. Genes which occupy similar positions on homologous chromosomes and control the same character are called **alleles**.

Mendel's conclusions according to modern genetics

As each chromosome is represented twice in the normal diploid cell, each gene must be represented twice. During meiosis, each one of a pair of homologous chromosomes passes into a separate gamete. Each gamete therefore contains one gene for each characteristic. Random fusion of gametes occurs during fertilization and the diploid number of chromosomes is restored. The zygote now formed has two genes controlling each characteristic. Where the members of the gene pair are alike (**AA**) the individual is described as **homozygous** for that character. Where the genes are different (**Aa**) it is **heterozygous** (**A** and **a** are alleles). The total genetic content of an organism or a cell is its **genotype** and may carry thousands of gene pairs affecting all aspects of the organism's development and activity. The observed condition of the organism is its **phenotype**.

Mendel's Law of Segregation can be expressed in modern terms:

'Of a pair of genes, only one passes into a gamete. It behaves independently of the other genes and passes intact from one generation to the next. It may or may not produce an effect depending upon whether it is dominant or recessive.'

Mendel's experiments can be written out diagramatically as shown on p188. This is the correct way to describe a genetic situation or problem and must always be used in questions which ask *'Describe or explain fully how . . .'* As a rule always begin by stating which allele is dominant and which is recessive. Use the initial letter of the dominant gene as the

188 Biology

genotypic symbol and its capital form (e.g. **T**) for dominant, and ordinary form (e.g. **t**) for recessive. Always include all the stages such as parental phenotype, parental genotype, etc., in your explanation (*see worked example p191*). This may be shown diagramatically as below.

Let **T** = dominant gene for tallness.
Let **t** = recessive gene for dwarfness.

P_1 Parental phenotypes   Pure tall   x   Pure dwarf
    Parental genotypes (2n)   TT   tt

Meiosis

Gametes (n)   T   T   t   t

Random fertilization

F_1 1st filial generation
    Genotypes (2n)   Tt   Tt   Tt   Tt

Phenotypes   All tall, heterozygous (genes **T** and **t** remain distinct in spite of dominance of **T**)

The F_1 generation were allowed to fertilize.

F_1 Phenotypes (2n)   Tall   x   Tall
    Genotypes   Tt   Tt
                         (self
Meiosis   fertilisation)

Gametes (n)   T   t   T   t

Random fertilization

F_2 Genotypes (2n)   TT   Tt   tT   tt
                        homozygous   heterozygous

                        heterozygous   homozygous
                             Tall   Dwarf
    Phenotypes   3   :   1

This ratio of 3 : 1 is called the **monohybrid ratio** because only one pair of contrasting characters is being considered.

The above explanation may be used directly in answering questions such as the following, where the F_2 phenotypes show an approximate 3 : 1 ratio.

The seeds resulting from a cross between a tall pea plant and a dwarf one produced plants all of which were tall. When these plants were allowed to self-pollinate, the resulting seeds produced 908 tall plants and 293 dwarf plants. Using symbols and a written explanation, account fully for these results. What would be the results of interbreeding the dwarf plants? (16)

[LOND]

Backcross This is an experimental technique used to determine the genotype of an organism, e.g. the genotype of a long winged *Drosophila* may be homozygous (**LL**) or heterozygous (**Ll**). In order to establish which, the fly is backcrossed with a double recessive (**ll**) vestigial (short) winged fly. If the offspring are all long winged, the unknown parental genotype is homozygous dominant. A ratio of 1 long : 1 vestigial wing indicates a heterozygote, e.g.

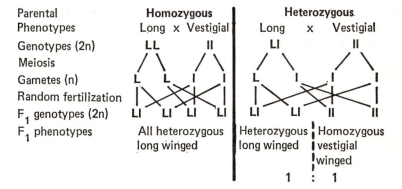

Incomplete dominance This condition occurs where two or more alleles do not show complete dominance and recessiveness. In most cases where this occurs the heterozygote has a phenotype which is intermediate between the homozygous dominant and recessive conditions. Two examples are given.

Example 1 In some plant species a red flowered plant crossed with a white flowered plant produces an F_1 generation with all pink flowers. Neither the red nor the white allele is dominant. When self-fertilized, the F_2 progeny are in the ratio of 1 red : 2 pink : 1 white.

Let **R** = red allele, and **W** = white allele.

| P_1 | Phenotypes | Pure red × Pure white |
| | Genotypes (2n) | RR   WW |

Meiosis

Gametes (n)

Random fertilization

| F_1 | Genotypes (2n) | RW RW RW RW |
| | Phenotypes | All pink (intermediate character as a result of incomplete dominance) |

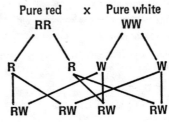

| F_1 | Phenotypes | Pink × Pink |
| | Genotypes (2n) | RW (self fertilise) RW |

Meiosis

Gamètes (n)

Random fertilization

F_2	Genotypes (2n)	RR RW WR WW
	Phenotypes	Red Pink Pink White
		1 : 2 : 1

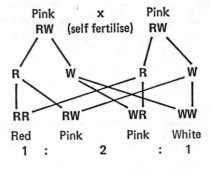

Example 2 Inheritance of blood groups in man is controlled by a group of three alleles **A**, **B** and **O**. This is the **multiple allele** condition, and shows incomplete dominance with regard to two alleles **A** and **B**. A person may only possess two such alleles (one on each of a pair of homologous chromosomes). **A** and **B** are equally dominant, **O** is recessive to both **A** and **B**.

Table 10.1 Genetics of blood groups in man

Possible genotype	Phenotype
AA homozygous	Group **A**
AO heterozygous	
BB homozygous	Group **B**
BO heterozygous	
AB incomplete dominance	Group **AB**
OO homozygous recessive	Group **O**

It is possible for two parents of blood group **A** and **B** respectively to produce children exhibiting all phenotypes.

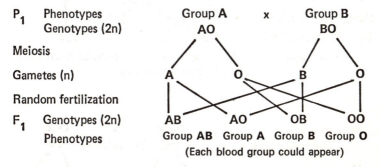

Genetics problems involving the inheritance of blood groups are very common. Using the information given above try to answer the following question.

Explain fully how two people of blood group 'A' may have three children all of whom are blood group 'O'. [13]   (o)

Sex determination in mammals

This is determined genetically as shown below. Female body cells have 23 pairs of chromosomes of which one pair are both **X** chromosomes. Male body cells have 23 pairs of chromosomes, one of which contains an **X** and a **Y** chromosome. All eggs contain an **X** chromosome. 50% of sperms containing an **X** chromosome and 50% contain a **Y** chromosome. The sex of the offspring depends upon which type of sperm fertilizes the egg.

	Female	Male
P_1 Phenotypes	Female	Male
Genotypes (2n)	XX	XY

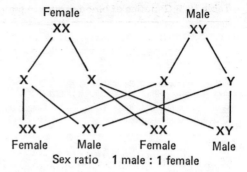

Sex ratio 1 male : 1 female

Sex linkage

This may not be required for your examination. Check this on the syllabus or ask your teacher before going through it. Genes which are

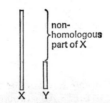

Fig. 10.3 Sex linkage

located on the sex chromosomes but do not determine sex characteristics are said to be **sex-linked**. They are inherited along with the sex of the organism. In the male (**XY**), the **Y** chromosome is homologous with

Table 10.2 Sex linkage in haemophilia

Possible phenotypes		Possible genotypes
Female	normal	XX
	normal but carrier	XX^h
	haemophiliac	X^{h}X^h
Male	normal	XY
	haemophiliac	X^{h}Y

only a small portion of the X chromosome. The non-homologous part of the **X** chromosome can therefore carry genes which the **Y** chromosome cannot. The effects of either dominant or recessive genes will appear in the phenotype. Sex linked characteristics occur more frequently in males since they appear in the phenotype even when present in the heterozygous condition, i.e., X^hY. In the female the presence of a single recessive gene (**h**) will be masked by the normal dominant gene on the homologous **X** chromosome (XX^h). Another common example of this is the inheritance of red/green colour blindness.

Variation

This term is used to describe the infinite number of combinations of characteristics seen among individuals of the same species.

Phenotypic variation (variation in physical characteristics of the organism) is determined by genotype but may be modified by the environment, e.g. the basic body shape and size in man is inherited but final size can be modified by environmental factors such as quantity of food eaten, exercise, disease, etc.

Genotype – each organism produced by sexual reproduction has a unique genotype. Differences in the composition and combinations of genes between individuals result from mutations and genetic reassortment. Genotypic variation forms the basis for natural selection in the process of evolution.

Environment – environmental conditions, e.g. temperature, light, water, food availability, disease, etc., may allow or prevent the full expression of the genotype, e.g. adding fertilizers to soil can increase crop yield.

Differences in physical characteristics (phenotypic variation) can be measured, e.g. index-finger length, height, blood group, ability to roll tongue, etc. When these results are examined they are seen to fall into two categories.

1 Continuous variation

The height of a large group of children of same age and sex is taken and the results plotted as shown on the graph in Fig. 10.4. This type of smooth curve is called a normal distribution curve. The highest point represents the average height and there are as many very tall people as very short people.

This is **continuous** variation. Characteristics showing this pattern of variation are controlled by several genes and influenced by environmental factors, e.g. weight in man, seed number and fruit size in tomato.

These characteristics are non-heritable, i.e. they are not passed on to their offspring.

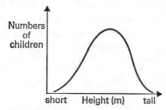

Fig. 10.4 Distribution curve for height

2 Discontinuous variation

Here there is an abrupt jump from one characteristic to another. There are no intermediates. In **discontinuous** variation the characteristics are controlled by one or a few major genes. Environmental factors have no effect on them and they are passed on to the next generation, i.e. they are heritable (e.g. blood groups, sex of individual).

Variations between individuals are either continuous or discontinuous. From the list below, select one example of each type of variation and place the letter in the correct column of the table.

A presence of ear lobes
B rate of heartbeat
C length of handspan
D ability to roll tongue
E colour of iris

Continuous variation	Discontinous variation

[2] (SCE)

Sources of variation

1 Mutation This is a sudden change in either the amount or structure of the chromosomal material (DNA). A change in the amount of DNA produces a chromosome mutation, e.g. in mongolism each cell has 47 chromosomes instead of the normal 46. A change in the structure of DNA produces a gene mutation, e.g. haemophilia. Mutations are rare and usually occur during cell division (mitosis or meiosis). Their rate can be increased by X-rays, ultra-violet rays, radioactivity (α, β, γ rays), and chemicals such as mustard gas, nicotine, tar and some drugs. Whilst most mutations are recessive (*see* p184) and harmful they do provide the main source of genetic variation within the population – the raw material of evolution.

2 Genetic reassortment This results from the rearrangement of genes during meiosis in gamete formation and from the random fusion of gametes at fertilization.

Using the information given above construct an answer that contains ten clear points that would give full marks on this question.

What are the main causes of variation within a species? [10]   (O & C)

Prevention of variation
In some cases identical organisms can be produced naturally, e.g. identical twins, asexual reproduction in plants and animals, or artificially as in cloning and tissue culture.

Identical twins Separation of the daughter cells formed at the first division of the fertilized egg, and their subsequent development by repeated mitotic divisions produces two embryos. Since they are formed from the same egg cell both embryos will possess identical sets of chromosomes.

Cloning This is the process of growing new multicellular organisms from a single cell. Any cell of the body, other than a gamete, if given the right conditions, will develop by mitosis into a new organism. Single cells from one organism will each produce an organism with an identical genotype (e.g. a single carrot cell has been used to produce a new carrot plant identical to the parent).

Evolution

The occurrence of variation within a species means that some individuals will be better suited to living in the environment than others. Charles Darwin recognized this as the basis of the process by which new species arise from pre-existing forms. In 1859 he published a book called *On the Origin of Species by means of Natural Selection*. In it he recognized the process of evolution, he presented data demonstrating it, and he developed a theory of how evolution took place. His theory is based on the following three observations.

1 **Organisms tend to produce as many offspring as possible.**
2 **The number of individuals in a species remains remarkably constant.**
3 **Variation exists among members of a species.**

From 1 and 2 he concluded that there exists, within nature, a *struggle for survival*. Some organisms survive and reproduce whilst others do not. Darwin's studies of variation (observation 3) suggested that those organisms best adapted phenotypically to the environment survived, reproduced and passed on their advantageous characteristics to their offspring. By this means the ever-changing environment continuously selects those organisms best fitted for survival (survival of the fittest). This forms the basis of evolution by **natural selection.**

Examples of natural selection

1 Mutations These occur in insects making them resistant to pesticides. New pesticides were produced to kill these mutants.

Insects breed very quickly and have a high mutation rate. Some of these new mutations gave the insects resistance to the newly-developed pesticides.

2 Industrial melanism The normal form of the peppered moth (*Biston betularia*) possesses pale mottled wings resembling a peppery pattern. Robins, thrushes and other birds prey on the moths by plucking them from the surfaces of trees. In 1848 a melanic (dark) mutant appeared in Manchester. In smoke-polluted areas (e.g. Manchester) the melanic form is well camouflaged when resting on the soot-covered trees, whereas the normal form is easily seen and more frequently preyed upon by birds. Therefore dark colour provides a selective advantage in this environment.

In non-polluted areas the reverse is true and the melanic forms are more easily seen and preyed upon (selective predation). Therefore the normal form still predominates here.

Current figures: Manchester 99% melanic form;

N. Scotland (unpolluted) 99% normal form.

These proportions have remained relatively stable from one year to the next for some time.

Formation of new species

Isolation is a factor in producing evolutionary change. It separates a population of a species into two or more groups. No exchange of genes occurs between the separated groups. Mutation and selection take place independently within each group and new species may develop (*see* Fig. 10.5).

Genetics and evolution 197

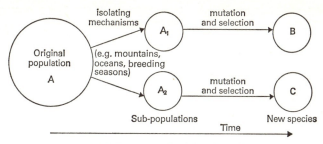

Fig. 10.5 Summary of species formation

Evidence for evolution
1 From **palaeontology** – the study of fossils provides evidence of gradual changes from one type of organism to another having taken place over a long period of time, e.g. evolution of horse.
2 From **geographical distribution** – some of the animals on the Galapagos Islands are distinct in certain ways from similar species found on the mainland and other islands. These organisms had a common ancestor. When geographical isolation of the islands occurred, no interbreeding could take place. Mutation and genetic reassortment followed by natural selection produced the range of closely related but distinct species seen today, e.g. the Galapagos' finches.
3 From **comparative anatomy** – similar structures are found in many organisms and this suggests that they have evolved from a common ancestor which possessed these structures, e.g. the basic plan of the limb bones is the same in nearly all vertebrates (pentadactyl limb). It has been considerably modified in many vertebrates and put to different uses, e.g. bat – flying; mole – digging; horse – running; whale – swimming.
4 From **embryology** – the study of the development of the embryos of related organisms, e.g. the vertebrates, shows remarkable similarities. This evidence suggests that they had a common ancestor.
5 From **genetics** (artificial selection) – by **selective breeding** techniques man has successfully reared improved varieties of animals and plants, e.g. Jersey cows with increased milk yield, seedless oranges, etc. In each case man has replaced natural selection with artificial selection and determined which organisms should be allowed to breed in order to obtain the desired characteristics.

198 Biology

Most of the questions set on evolution are very straightforward and only require a thorough understanding of the information given above, e.g.

(a) *Give an account of the theory of evolution by natural selection.* [10]
(b) *Outline the types of evidence which suggest that evolution has occurred.* [10] (O & C)

Key words

Mendel
characters
pure breeding
recessive
dominant
segregation
chromosomes
deoxyribonucleic
  acid
gene
homologous
  chromosomes
alleles

homozygous
heterozygous
genotype
phenotype
monohybrid ratio
backcross
incomplete
  dominance
multiple allele
sex-linked
variation
continuous
discontinuous

mutation
genetic reassortment
cloning
evolution
natural selection
industrial melanism
isolation
palaeontology
geographical
  distribution
comparative anatomy
embryology
selective breeding

Past examination questions

1 *In human beings the allele (B) for brown eyes is dominant to the allele (b) for blue eyes. If a brown-eyed man marries a blue-eyed woman, and they have six children, all brown eyed, what are the possible genotypes of all the family, (i) father, (ii) mother, (iii) children?* [4] (JMB)

2 (a) *In a wild population some mice were light in colour and others were dark. Owls killed 40% of the light-coloured and 10% of the dark-coloured mice. Using this as an example, explain what is meant by the term 'natural selection'.*
  (b) *Suppose there is an isolated population of light-coloured mice. Is there any possibility that their descendants will be darker in colour? Give the reason for your answer.*
  (c) *A mouse with ears 15 mm long was mated with a mouse with ears 12 mm long. The offspring had ears of different lengths between*

12 and 15 mm. What does this tell you about the inheritance of ear length in these mice? (AEB)

3 *Assuming that hair length in a mammal (not human) is controlled by one pair of alleles, show how two long-haired parents could produce a short-haired offspring.* [7] (JMB)

4 (a) *Name, or very briefly describe, a single pair of contrasted genetic characters which show incomplete dominance.* [2]
  (b) *Name the organism in which these characters occur.* [1]
  (c) *Give one example of an environmental factor which can cause phenotypic variation.* [1] (O)

5 *Explain, using appropriate genetic symbols, the results from crosses between* (a) *a homozygous tall plant and a homozygous dwarf plant,* [6] (b) *two heterozygous tall plants,* [6] (c) *a heterozygous tall plant and a homozygous dwarf plant.* [6] *In all these crosses assume that tall is dominant to dwarf.* (LOND)

6 (a) *What do you understand by the terms, (i) evolution; (ii) variation; (iii) natural selection?* [9]
  (b) *Describe one piece of evidence which suggests that evolution has taken place.* [6]
  (c) *Describe one piece of evidence which suggests that evolution is still occurring.* [5] (O & C)

11 Ecology and microbiology

Environment The surroundings in which an organism lives.
Ecosystem The living and non-living components of a region, which interact to produce a stable system.
Habitat The region in which an organism lives.
Capillarity The rise of water in narrow spaces due to molecular attraction.
Photoperiodism The response of a plant to the relative lengths of light and dark periods.
Producer An organism which synthesises complex organic compounds from simple inorganic materials.
Consumer An organism that takes in ready synthesized organic material.
Food chain A food relationship where energy is transferred from one group of organisms to another.
Pollution Unusually high levels of natural or unnatural constituents in the environment, which cause undesirable effects.
Vector An animal which transmits a pathogenic organism from one organism to another.
Symbiosis A relationship between two organisms which is of mutual benefit.

Ecology

Ecology is the study of the relationships between living organisms and their **environment**. There are three major environments, marine, freshwater and terrestrial, containing many **habitats**. The environment can be divided into two natural divisions – the **abiotic** or non-living environment and the **biotic** or living environment. These two interact in such a way as to produce a balanced system called the **ecosystem**.

Abiotic environment
The main features of the non-living environment concern the climate, nutrient cycles and the soil. These factors influence the number and distribution of organisms within a given area. Whilst primarily affecting plant growth they also affect the animals which feed on them and the whole balance of nature.

Light
The intensity and amount of light varies with seasons of the year, latitude and weather conditions. It is essential for green plants and they possess numerous adaptations for obtaining optimum illumination for photosynthesis (*see* chapter 3). Some plants (e.g. henbane) respond to long periods of daylight by flowering whilst others flower only when daylength is short. This response to light is termed **photoperiodism**. Light may also influence vegetative development of tubers, development of fruits and seeds, onset/break of **dormancy** in seeds and buds and **hibernation** and nesting in animals.

Water
Water is required by plants for photosynthesis and by all organisms for metabolism. Plants living in deserts must possess efficient adaptations to cope with such conditions, e.g. reduced number of stomata; thick waxy cuticle; water storage tissues.

Temperature
The rate of enzyme reactions and metabolism varies with temperature. All organisms live within a narrow temperature range and possess many physiological and behavioural adaptations to remain within these limits, e.g. hibernation in animals. Here the animal sleeps deeply as its body temperature and metabolic rate fall. In plants the rates of photosynthesis and water uptake vary with temperature.

Nutrient cycles
All living organisms depend upon adequate supplies of nutrients. Plants are able to synthesize food from these nutrients using energy from the Sun. Whilst the major nutrient elements (carbon, hydrogen, oxygen and nitrogen) are constantly cycled and recycled through ecosystems, energy is not.

Carbon cycle Carbon exists (a) as a component part of tissues of living organisms, (b) in natural and man-made organic compounds and (c) as carbon dioxide in the atmosphere (0.03–0.04%). Carbon dioxide is the source of carbon for all plants and therefore indirectly for all animals. Photosynthetic activity of green plants extracts the carbon and incorporates it into carbohydrates. Some of these carbohydrates are later converted into proteins and fat. Carbon is returned to the environment by respiration of all organisms and by decay of dead organisms. (*See* Fig. 11.1).

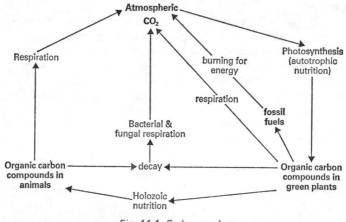

Fig. 11.1 Carbon cycle

Questions based on these nutrient cycles are common so learn them well.

Describe what is meant by the following: carbon cycle. (CAM)

Water cycle Water circulates between the atmosphere, land and sea, but a significant amount passes through living organisms. Water is a raw material of photosynthesis and a source of hydrogen and oxygen for all living organisms. Plants and animals return water to the atmosphere in many ways, including respiration.

Nitrogen cycle Nitrogen is necessary for the formation of protein. Air contains about 79% nitrogen but as a gas it is biologically inert and unavailable to most living organisms. It is absorbed by plant roots as nitrates from the soil and used for protein synthesis. Animals obtain their protein by eating plants.

Certain bacteria and fungi are capable of continually cycling nitrogen through the ecosystems as shown in Fig. 11.2.

Ecology and microbiology 203

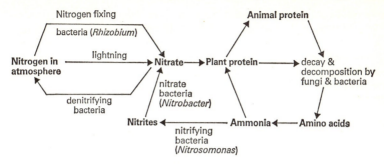

Fig. 11.2 Nitrogen cycle

The information given in Fig. 11.2 may be useful in answering questions such as,

Explain how the nitrogen of plant protein is changed, after the death of the plant, into a form which other plants can use. [5] (JMB)
(*See also* question 1 on p219).

Soils
Typically they are composed of the following constituents:

1 Mineral particles of different sizes
2 Water
3 Air
4 Dissolved mineral salts
5 Humus
6 Micro-organisms
7 Other soil-dwelling organisms (e.g. earthworms)

The above are all points which should be learnt and related to the part they play in soil fertility, e.g.

List the living and non-living components of a well-balanced soil. Explain the contribution of each component to soil fertility [10, 15] (LOND)

1 **Mineral particles** are formed from weathered rocks. Their size and nature determines the character of the soil. This in turn dictates which plant and animal species may live there. The crumb structure of a soil depends on the proportions of clay, sand and humus. Sandy

soils with predominantly large particles are light, warm and easy to cultivate. They have a loose texture and afford poor support for roots and are susceptible to wind erosion. Rapid drainage in these soils leaves them deficient in salts. Clay soils are heavy, cold and hard to work. The small particles are closely packed hindering drainage and decreasing air spaces. Fertile soils are generally **loams** consisting of mixtures of different types of particle.

Experiment *To investigate the composition of soil by sedimentation.*

Method Shake a sample of soil with water in a measuring cylinder and then allow the soil to settle out (**sedimentation**) as shown in Fig. 11.3. Calculate the percentage of each component.

Results

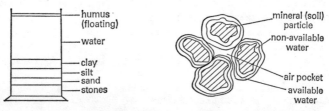

Fig. 11.3 The composition of soil   *Fig. 11.4* Soil water

Conclusion Roughly equal proportions of all major components are present. This is called loam – a rich type of soil.

2 **Water** adheres to soil particles as a thin film and is held there by **capillary attraction** and chemical forces. The water content of a soil varies according to external conditions and the nature of the soil. Soil water may be (Fig. 11.4)
  (a) available water – capillary water which can be absorbed by plant roots, and drainage water remaining in the soil after rain,
  (b) non-available water – roots cannot exert sufficient force to remove and absorb this water by osmosis.
3 **Air** fills the spaces between mineral and organic particles in soil which is not waterlogged. The size of the air spaces depends on the size of the particles. This affects drainage. Larger air spaces allow more rapid drainage, but reduce capillarity. The soil atmosphere is very similar to atmospheric air but usually there is less oxygen and more

Ecology and microbiology 205

carbon dioxide (why?). The oxygen of the air is used for aerobic respiration by plant root tissues, and other soil dwelling organisms.

Experiment *To determine the proportion of air in soil.*

Method Half fill a large measuring cylinder with water and note the level of the water. Fully immerse a tin in the water of the cylinder. Remove the tin plus water, and empty the water. Punch some holes in the base of the tin, and then drive the open end of the tin into the soil. Carefully remove the tin containing the soil sample, and level off the soil in it. Immerse the tin containing soil in the water of the cylinder. When no more bubbles of air escape from the tin, add water from another measuring cylinder until the original water level is reached.

Results Volume of water added = volume of air in soil.

4 **Mineral salts** comprise 0.2% by weight of the soil content. They originate from the decomposition of plant and animal remains and from their waste products. They exist as a dilute solution in soil water and are essential for healthy plant growth (*see* p45). They affect the pH of the soil and therefore determine which plants can survive there.

Experiment *To determine soil pH.*

Method and results Allow 1 g of soil to soak in universal indicator solution and distilled water in an evaporating dish for 3 minutes. Drain off the solution, compare its colour with the universal indicator colour chart and read off the pH.

5 **Humus** is composed of the remains of dead organisms and their waste products. It is formed at the soil surface and mixed into the soil by earthworm activity and ploughing. Bacterial decay of humus releases the soluble nitrates and other mineral salts required for plant growth. Humus can improve the texture of soils, e.g. if added to heavy soils it improves aeration, and if added to light soils it prevents loss of salts (**leaching**) by too rapid drainage.

Experiment *To determine water and humus content of soil.*

Method for water content Weigh an evaporating basin, add the soil sample and reweigh. Heat basin plus sample in an oven (at a temperature between 100–120 °C) for 24 hours to drive off soil water. Cool in a desiccator, weigh. Continue heating and reweighing until two weighings give identical readings.

Results and calculations
(initial soil + basin weight) − basin weight = initial soil weight
(final soil + basin weight) − basin weight = final soil weight
initial weight of soil − final weight of soil = weight of water present

$$\frac{\text{weight of water}}{\text{initial weight of soil}} \times 100 = \% \text{ water in soil sample}$$

Method for humus content Place the basin plus a known weight of dry soil from the above experiment on a tripod and gauze and heat it strongly in a Bunsen flame to burn off the humus. Cool in a desiccator and weigh. Continue heating and reweighing until two weighings give identical readings. Loss of weight here is the weight of humus originally present.

Results and calculations
weight of dry soil − weight of strongly heated soil = weight of humus

$$\frac{\text{weight of humus}}{\text{initial weight of soil}} \times 100 = \% \text{ humus in soil sample}$$

Using the information given above check that you are able to answer this question.

For a sample of soil describe precisely how you would determine:
(i) the percentage by mass of the water content, and
(ii) the percentage by volume of the air content of a sample of soil.
Explain any calculations you would have to make from your measurements.
[7, 7] (o)

6 **Micro-organisms** include bacteria and fungi. They break down organic compounds and humus to release soluble salts which are absorbed in solution by plant roots. (*NB* De-nitrifying bacteria break down humus to release substances virtually useless to living organisms (*see* p215).)

7 **Earthworms** contribute to the maintenance of soil fertility in several ways. Their burrowing activity allows air into the soil and easy penetration of root systems. During feeding they ingest fine particles of soil from underground which is broken up in their gizzard. Much of it is eventually redeposited at the soil surface providing a

good **tilth** for seed germination. Earthworms drag dead leaves and other organic remains below ground where they are decomposed more quickly by microbes.

All the above factors contribute to the fertility of soil. The 'ideal' soil is light in texture, warm, rich in dissolved salts and plentifully supplied with water, but not waterlogged. A loam meets most of these conditions.

Agricultural practices

Manuring The continual harvesting of crops removes large amounts of mineral salts from the soil. These must be replaced to maintain soil fertility. This can be done by a system of manuring. (a) Organic manures (animal faeces, green manures and compost) are derived from dead plant and waste animal materials. They contain many if not all of the necessary elements for plant growth. They decay slowly, add humus and minerals to the soil and are best ploughed in in the autumn; (b) Inorganic manures are now widely used. They are relatively simple chemical substances which contain the necessary elements for plant growth. Advantages of inorganic manures are (i) quick acting when dissolved, (ii) can supply one particular mineral which is deficient, and (iii) easy to apply. Disadvantages include (i) high cost, (ii) precipitate colloidal particles of soil and decrease water retention capacity, (iii) contain no humus, and (iv) if not used carefully, may upset mineral balance of soil and its **crumb structure**.

Ploughing In spring this (a) increases surface area for water evaporation; (b) crumbles soil, good for seed germination; and (c) aerates soil stimulating microbial activity.

In autumn this (a) mixes manure into soil where it decomposes rapidly; (b) furrows prevent water run-off; and (c) frost penetrates easily, kills pests, weathers clods of earth, provides better soil texture.

Liming The addition of lime (a) flocculates (clumps) the small particles of clay soils, so aiding drainage and improving aeration; (b) neutralizes acid soils, and (c) kills unwanted pests.

Crop rotation Different crops follow one another on a given piece of ground in successive years in a definite pre-arranged order. e.g. Norfolk rotation. This is a four year rotation:

| 1 Clover (leguminous crop) | 2 Wheat | 3 Root crop (turnips, swedes) | 4 Barley |

Clover finishes growth in autumn; is ploughed in and wheat sown later that autumn. Wheat crop harvested in following late summer. Land then ploughed deeply and left during winter. In following spring it is cultivated and a root crop is sown in May. Root crop receives most manures for the rotation. It is harvested in the following winter. Barley is then sown the following spring.

Advantages (a) Clover brings about increase in nitrate content of soil because of activity of nitrogen-fixing bacteria in root nodules. (b) Disease/damage less likely since most pests are specific for one particular crop. (c) Weeds more easily kept down when rotation occurs. (d) Economical on manure. Also some crops are deeper rooted and draw mineral ions from sub-soil whilst others are shallow rooted. In this way ions at different soil levels are utilized. (e) Labour requirements spread throughout the year, since different crops have different seasons for sowing and harvesting.

Biotic environment

The abiotic environment supports living organisms (biotic factors) and determines their number and distribution. Energy is needed for the constant recycling of materials within an ecosystem. It is lost as it flows through the ecosystem and must be replaced by energy from the Sun.

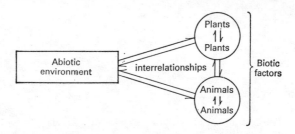

Fig. 11.5 Interactions within an ecosystem

Only green plants can utilize solar energy which is incorporated into sugars by photosynthesis. Plants are able to build up proteins, fat and vitamins from sugars. They are thus called the **producers** of the ecosystem. All animals (**consumers**) derive their energy for growth and

Ecology and microbiology 209

metabolism from producers. These feeding relationships can be summarized as a **food chain** (Fig. 11.6) where each stage of the chain is known as a **trophic level**. Microbial consumers which aid decay of dead organic matter at all levels are called **decomposers**.

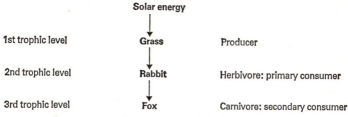

Fig. 11.6 A food chain

It is rare to find a simple food chain in an ecosystem. Usually there are several organisms at each level which may obtain food from any one of the lower levels. These complex feeding interrelationships are called **food webs**, e.g. fresh water crustacea are eaten by a variety of fish and amphibia (Fig. 11.7).

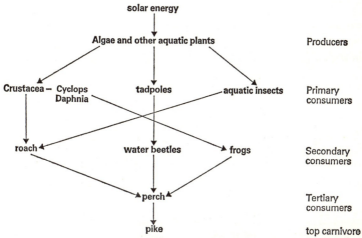

Fig. 11.7 Food web in a freshwater pond

Only 1% of the total energy that reaches the plant as light is incorporated into plant tissues. As energy is passed along the food chain there is about a 90% loss between each level. These energy losses are accounted for in Fig. 11.8, and explain why there are rarely more than five trophic levels.

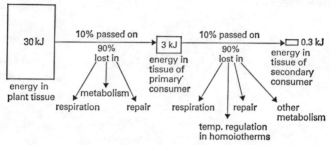

Fig. 11.8 Energy flow through food chain

Pyramid of numbers

There is generally an increase in size (mass) of organism from primary consumer to the final carnivores in the food chain, but a decrease in number (Fig. 11.9). As there is a decrease in available energy at each

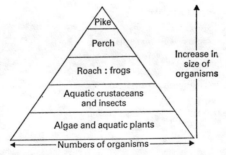

Fig. 11.9 Pyramid of biomass (amount of living material)

successive link in the food chain there must be a corresponding decrease in the amount of living material that it can sustain.

Variation in numbers within a population

Populations of organisms fluctuate in response to changing conditions within an ecosystem, but over a long period of time the average size of each population remains the same.

If the predators become too numerous they will deplete the numbers of herbivores. Then the predator number will decline because of food shortage. Subsequently, with fewer predators the herbivore numbers will again begin to rise (Fig. 11.10). (What will happen to the vegetation in this ecosystem?)

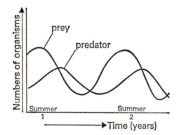

Fig. 11.10 Predator/prey interactions

Thus over a period of time there is a general balance in numbers of **predator** and **prey**. It is not an absolutely steady state and is often referred to as a state of **dynamic equilibrium** in the ecosystem (*see* question 3(c), p219).

Man and his environment

As man's industrial and technological ability has advanced, so has his ability to manipulate the environment. His remarkable success in combating disease and exploiting natural resources has led to a vast increase in the size of his population. The growth curve of the population takes the form of an **exponential curve** (Fig. 11.11).

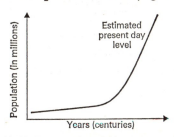

Fig. 11.11 Growth of world human population

Inevitably the curve must flatten out at some stage in the future or the population will outstrip food resources. Improved methods of food production will help this problem but the only solution must be a reduction in birth rate. The increase in human population has meant that man has affected his environment in two major ways – exploitation of natural resources and industrialization.

Exploitation of natural resources

1 Effects of agriculture. **Monoculture** (concentrated growing of a single species of plant in one area) is the major method of crop production today. However, high densities of crops provide optimum conditions for pests and spread of disease.
2 Use of **pesticides** (especially **insecticides**). Though effective, it is expensive and can kill many other organisms which are harmless to man's crops so upsetting the balance of the ecosystem. They may kill the pest's natural enemies, thus removing a form of biological control of the pests. Non-degradable pesticides (e.g. DDT) can accumulate within the tissues of organisms and be passed along food chains where they become increasingly concentrated. Animals at the end of the food chain may receive a dose large enough to be fatal.
3 Use of **herbicides**. They remove weeds from crops but can upset the ecosystem by removing a food source or habitat of other organisms.

Using the information given in this chapter, and examples from your notes and textbook, think out an answer to this question.

Quoting named organisms, describe what effects the following can have on food chains: (i) pollution, (ii) insecticides. [5, 5]   (O & C)

Man is becoming increasingly aware of the harm he has caused to the environment. The general public is now being encouraged by education and law to be much more careful in the exploitation of the land. By studying the life cycle, behaviour and predators of a pest man is attempting to avoid the use of pesticides.

Example 1 Eradicating mosquitoes in tropical countries by draining swamps and spraying stagnant water with oil. *Think out what effect these measures will have on the mosquito.*

Example 2 **Biological control**. Introducing a natural enemy of the pest into the habitat, e.g. in Australia the prickly pear cactus thrived and invaded many pasturelands. Larvae of a moth which feed on the prickly pear were introduced, and the spread of the prickly pear was controlled within 10 years.

Ecology and microbiology

Effects of industrialization
The following notes cover the main points but you should consult your own notes and textbook for further details.

1 Depletion of areas of natural vegetation to make room for housing, factories, roads, etc.
2 Depletion of non-replaceable resources for energy and by industry.
3 Over-exploitation of replaceable materials, e.g. timber, wood.

The major anxiety caused by industrialization is however, pollution of the atmosphere, soil and water. The main factors in this are (a) the release of chemical wastes from industrial processes, (b) use of pesticides and herbicides, (c) accumulation of unwanted materials (rubbish), and increasingly (d) disposal of radioactive waste.

Air pollution Caused by dust, smoke, soot, sulphur dioxide from burning fossil fuels. Reduced by Clean Air Act (1956). Combustion engines produce carbon monoxide, lead and nitrogen oxides – all serious health hazards. Radioactive materials may enter the ground via rain and be concentrated by food chains.

$$\text{strontium 90} \to \text{soil} \to \text{grass} \to \text{cattle} \begin{matrix} \nearrow \text{milk} \searrow \\ \searrow \text{cheese} \nearrow \end{matrix} \text{man (can produce leukaemia)}$$

Water pollution Industrial and domestic wastes enter inland waterways and sea. Oil spillage at sea kills wildlife and damages sea-shores. Detergents, sewage and fertilizers encourage algal, bacterial and fungal growth. They use up oxygen which animals need. Legislation now being introduced to limit these problems.

Soil pollution Caused by dumping of rubbish and chemicals. Aesthetic problem and health hazard.

Conservation
The means of preventing over-exploitation of plants and animals, and to preserve the stability of ecosystems. This can be achieved in several ways:

1 **Legislation.** (a) Many species threatened with extinction may be protected by the law, e.g. Protection of Birds Act, 1954 (b). Since the Clean Air Act, many species have returned to industrialized areas.

(c) Local authorities can pass by-laws to prevent removal of wild flowers from the environment. (d) Nature reserves protect endangered species which live there, e.g. Brownsea Island Bird Sanctuary. (e) National parks have been created which preserve areas of outstanding beauty and protect them from over-exploitation.

2 **Recycling of materials.** Many waste manufactured components are now being efficiently **recycled**, e.g. old cars can be packaged and sent to factories which recover some of the metal for re-use.
3 Systems of power use are being developed which utilize the inexhaustible supplies of solar and wave energy.
4 **Reclamation.** Many schemes are in existence which are **reclaiming** derelict land, e.g. (a) The NCB has an efficient organization for the restoration of land used for open cast coal mining. (b) Local authorities with government finance have landscaped derelict land in an effort to raise the quality of the environment under their control, e.g. Lower Swansea Valley Project.

Having read of the effects of man's activities on the environment, draw up an essay plan for the following question.

Describe some of (a) the beneficial, and (b) the detrimental effects of man's activities on the environment. [25] (LOND)

Microbiology

This is the study of bacteria, fungi and viruses.

Bacteria
The cell wall is composed of protein and fatty substances. It may be covered by a slime capsule and possess flagella. There is no vacuole

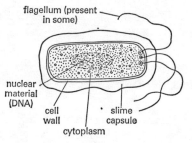

Fig. 11.12 Structure of a bacterium

Ecology and microbiology

present within the cytoplasm, however most of the common cell organelles are present with the exception of mitochondria. Nuclear material is present but is not bounded by a nuclear membrane (*see* Fig. 11.12).

Bacteria may have a variety of shapes such as irregular collections of spherical cells, e.g. *Staphylococcus* (causing boils); straight cylindrical rods, e.g. *Bacillus* (causing tuberculosis); curved cylindrical rods, e.g. *Vibrio* (causing cholera).

Study the following question before proceeding to revise the effect of bacteria on man and the ecosystem.

(a) *Briefly describe the structure of (i) a bacterium, and (ii) a virus.* [6]
(b) *Name one disease caused by each and describe how each organism is transmitted to a new host.* [4]
(c) *What part do bacteria play in the cycling of materials under natural conditions?* [10]
(d) *How would you control bacterial activities in order to preserve food?* [5] (o)

Role as decomposers in recycling nutrients

Saprophytic bacteria produce enzymes which digest organic material externally, then absorb the products into the cytoplasm. They produce humus from plant and animal remains and cause **putrefaction**. In this way they enable recycling of materials to take place.

1 **Decay** (putrefying) **bacteria** break down protein of dead organic matter to release ammonia which combines with other substances in the soil to form ammonium compounds.
2 **Nitrifying bacteria** obtain their energy by oxidation of ammonium compounds to form nitrites. The nitrite is oxidized to nitrate which then becomes available for absorption by plant roots.
3 **Nitrogen-fixing bacteria** may be free-living, e.g. *Azobacter*, or living symbiotically in root nodules of beans, peas, clover, e.g. *Rhizobium*. They can convert atmospheric nitrogen gas into ammonium compounds which other bacteria convert into nitrates.
4 **Denitrifying bacteria** flourish in waterlogged soil and reduce nitrates to nitrogen gas which is lost from the soil (*see* nitrogen cycle p203).

Pathogenic (disease-producing) bacteria

Parasitic bacteria enter the tissues of a host and are **pathogenic** because of the poisonous waste (toxin) they produce when multiplying.

Examples of bacterial diseases are cholera, gonorrhoea, pneumonia, tetanus, typhoid, whooping cough.

Fungi

Fungi play an important role in decomposition and recycling. Saprophytic fungi feeding on dead organic matter digest food material extracellularly (*see* p58). Some of the simpler soluble materials formed are absorbed by the fungi, but much of it becomes available for absorption by plant roots.

Viruses

They are very small simple structures varying in shape and lacking a nucleus, cytoplasm and cell membrane (Fig. 11.13). Viruses are inert,

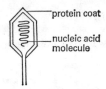

Fig. 11.13 Structure of a virus (simplified)

highly infectious particles causing a variety of diseases, e.g. smallpox, influenza, mumps, polio.

Life-cycle of a virus It attaches to the wall or membrane of host cell and breaks it down by enzyme action. The viral nucleic acid is squeezed into the host cell and causes it to produce new viral nucleic acid and in some cases the protein coat. Many viruses may be formed before they are released from the cell. The whole process may only take 30 minutes. In this way millions of viruses are produced in a short time and produce the symptoms of their particular infection.

Prevention of disease

Chemotherapy The use of chemicals to treat and cure disease. These may be manufactured drugs (e.g. mepacrine to cure malaria) or natural or synthetic antibiotics (e.g. penicillin extracted from the mould *Penicillium* and used to control many kinds of bacteria).

Food preservation (i) **Sterilization** – food is cooked at very high temperatures, canned or bottled and finally sealed whilst still very hot. Bacteria and fungi are killed by heat in excess of 100 °C, as are the more resistant spores. The seal prevents entry of any further microbes. (ii) **Pasteurization** – milk is heated to 72 °C for 15 seconds and quickly cooled to below 12 °C. This kills pathogenic bacteria, but other bacteria which survive can cause milk to turn sour and clot under appropriate conditions. (iii) **Refrigeration** – at low temperatures microbial activity is slow and they can neither cause appreciable decay nor multiply. (iv) **Dehydration** – food is dried. Microbes cannot survive without water, but their resistant spores can. They will begin to germinate immediately the food is moistened. (v) **Osmotic preservation** – food is immersed in concentrated solutions (brine or syrup). Microbes die in this situation because of loss of water. (vi) **Cooking** – prolonged heating of foods kills microbes and their resistant spores.

Associations between organisms
The three main associations are saprophytism, parasitism and symbiosis. They each form a way of life for several organisms and may affect man in a number of ways.

1 **Saprophytism** *See* p58 (*Mucor*) for details of this form of nutrition.

2 **Parasitism** *See* p59 for details of characteristics and the example, tapeworm. A good example of a plant parasite is the ectoparasite Dodder. This grows on nettles. Its stem possesses suckers (**haustoria**) which penetrate the host stem and its vascular bundles. It obtains water and synthesized organic substances from its host. It has no roots, and its leaves are unable to photosynthesize, therefore it is totally dependent on its host for food and water.

Trypanosoma (endoparasite) is a protozoan which causes African sleeping sickness, and is a useful example of a parasite involving an insect **vector**. The female tsetse fly bites an infected man and sucks his blood. It takes in the trypanosomes with its meal of blood. Within the insect the trypanosomes move from its gut to its salivary glands. When the fly bites another uninfected man, it injects the trypanosomes into his blood. Here they live, multiply and absorb nutrients from it. The toxic substances that are liberated as a result of their activity cause the sleeping sickness.

infected man → trypanosomes in tsetse fly → infects fit man
+ (trypanosomes)

3 Symbiosis An association between two organisms which is mutually beneficial to both, e.g. nitrogen-fixing bacteria living in nodules which they form in the roots of leguminous plants (clover). Within the nodule the bacteria fix atmospheric nitrogen into compounds which the plant can use to manufacture proteins (*see* p45). The bacteria gain carbohydrate from the host plant.

Key words

- environment
- habitat
- abiotic
- biotic
- ecosystem
- light
- photoperiodism
- dormancy
- hibernation
- nutrient cycle
- carbon cycle
- water cycle
- nitrogen cycle
- soils
- mineral particles
- loams
- sedimentation
- capillary attraction
- humus
- decay
- leaching
- micro-organisms
- tilth
- manures
- crumb structure
- ploughing
- liming
- crop rotation
- producers
- consumers
- food chain
- trophic level
- herbivore
- carnivore
- decomposers
- food web
- pyramid of numbers
- predators
- prey
- dynamic equilibrium
- exponential curve
- monoculture
- pesticides
- insecticides
- herbicides
- pollution
- biological control
- conservation
- recycling
- reclamation
- bacteria
- putrefaction
- decay bacteria
- nitrifying bacteria
- nitrogen fixing bacteria
- denitrifying bacteria
- pathogenic
- fungi
- viruses
- chemotherapy
- food preservation
- sterilization
- pasteurization
- refrigeration
- dehydration
- saprophytism
- parasitism
- symbiosis
- haustoria
- vector

Past examination questions

1 *Below is a simplified diagram of the cycle of nitrogen in nature:*

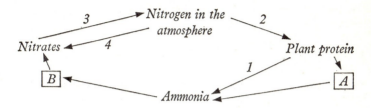

   (a) *Give the names of the substances in the boxes labelled A and B.*
   (b) *What processes or organisms are represented by the arrows numbered 1, 2, 3, 4?* (SCE)

2 (a) *What are the essential constituents of a fertile soil, and what are the functions of the inorganic fractions?*
   (b) *Describe briefly how you would improve the quality of an acid sandy soil in a garden.* (CAM)

3 *The figure shows a food web.*

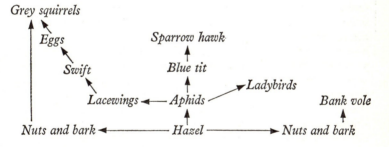

   (a) *What is the importance of the hazel in this web?*
   (b) *Name one carnivore and one herbivore in this web.*
   (c) *What might be the effect on the numbers of the ladybirds if the swifts were removed? Explain your answer.* (AEB)

4 *The caterpillar of the coconut moth may severely damage coconut trees by eating the leaves. The tachinid fly feeds and lives within the tissues of the coconut moth caterpillar. Where coconut moths cause great damage, the tachinid fly is introduced as a means of 'biological control'.*

(a) *Of the organisms in the relationship outlined above, which is (i) the parasite, (ii) the host, (iii) a herbivore?*
(b) *What is biological control?* (AEB)

5 (a) *Complete the following table of a food chain by naming suitable examples.* Producer
  Consumer 1
  Consumer 2
  Consumer 3
(b) *What is the source of energy in all food chains?* (AEB)

6 *Write short paragraphs on the biological significance of any five of the following topics:*

insecticides;   oil slicks in coastal waters;
biological control;   fungicides;
herbicides;   radioactive fallout;
eutrophication;   biodegradable packaging;
pollution indicators; the River Thames since 1964.* [5 × 4] (O & C)

7 *The spread of artificial fertilizer on soil is recommended at a rate of 100 g/m^2. To obtain the same supply of mineral salts requires a spread of compost of 5 kg/m^2.*
  (a) *Is the weight of compost required 5 times more, 50 times more or 500 times more than the weight of artificial fertilizer?*
  (b) *Name three soil organisms that help to convert compost into mineral salts.*
  (c) *Compost raises the temperature of soil. Describe one way in which it does so.*
  (d) *Why does crop yield increase with an increase in soil temperature?*
  (e) *Describe one other way, apart from raising of the temperature, in which the soil is improved after the addition of compost but not after the addition of artificial fertilizer.* (AEB)

12 Guide to examinations

Points to remember
Just as there is no foolproof way of revising there is no foolproof way of passing an examination. A conscientious effort throughout the course and adequate revision will certainly help on the examination day. There are so may factors which may impair your performance in examinations and a few simple points may help produce a better frame of mind for tackling the paper.

1 Do not tire yourself out with last minute cramming the day (or night) before the examination.
2 Get a good night's sleep and get up in good time for the exam.
3 Be sure you know which subject you are taking, what type of examination it will be, the time it begins and the room in which it will be held.
4 Arrive at the examination room with all the materials you will require, e.g. pens, pencils, ruler, eraser, etc., and your candidate number.
5 Allow yourself extra time to travel to school or college in case your bicycle has a puncture, etc.

These are all obvious points but every year many candidates enter the examination room either tired, late or in a panic because they had not considered them. Don't be one of these candidates.

When the examination begins there are several points which should be observed.

1 Read the instructions given at the beginning of the examination paper very carefully.
2 Answer all compulsory questions.

3 If the paper is divided into sections and a choice of questions is given within them ensure you answer the correct number from each section. Follow any advice given on how long to spend on each section.
4 Fill in your name, candidate number and centre number on all sheets as instructed.
5 Always answer the correct number of questions. Never decide to give three detailed answers in the time allocated if the instructions ask for four. The maximum number of marks to be obtained by this can only be 75%, and few people ever achieve full marks in an answer.
6 Most exam papers now give the distribution of marks for each question. Use this as a guide to how long you should spend on answering each part question or question.
7 Read through the questions and decide which you are going to answer. It is worth spending a few minutes over this and being certain you possess enough information to give complete answers. As a general rule begin by answering what is the easiest question for you or any compulsory questions. **Remember to stick to your time allocation**.
   (a) Answer the question which is set – do not rewrite to suit yourself.
   (b) Only give information which is relevant to the question. Do not write down all you know about that topic.
   (c) Examiners prefer answers which are concise and written in good English. Credit is sometimes given for orderly presentation.
8 Remember that the examiner is looking for the correct use of biological facts in your answer. Marks can only be awarded for what you write on the paper – not for what remains in your head.
9 Detail given on diagrams should not be repeated in words unless the diagram is making an answer more easily understood.
10 If you are running out of time in a question put down the important points in note form and do not worry about sentences. You may not gain full marks but you will gain some.
11 If time is available at the end of the examination read through your answers and correct any mistakes.

Question types
There are a variety of types of questions set at O level and you should know how to tackle those which will be used in your examinations.

1 Objective questions Answers are usually given in pencil on a special answer sheet and marked by machine. Between thirty and sixty questions are set – all are compulsory and vary in difficulty. This is a good way of testing your knowledge on all parts of the syllabus. So revise all topics.

Which one of the following formulae represents an amino acid?

A C_2H_5OH
B NH_4NO_3
C $C_{57}H_{104}O_6$
D NH_2CH_2COOH
E $C_6H_{12}O_6$ (LOND)

Only one of these choices (A–E) is correct. If you cannot tell which answer is correct try to eliminate the four which are incorrect. Usually three are easy to eliminate and you must work out which of those remaining is correct. This question is not testing your ability to remember formulae but the knowledge that all amino acids contain the elements C, H, O, N. Of the options, only B and D contain nitrogen and of these only D contains C, H, O, N. Answer therefore is D.

2 Short answer questions Answers are written on the question paper in spaces provided. This gives some indication of the length of answer required, e.g. sentence completion.

A muscle is attached to a bone by means of a . . . ., whereas two bones are joined together by . . . . (CAM)

In other cases a photograph, diagram, table, graph or passage is given and candidates are asked to answer several short questions, e.g.

In a mammal the eyes look steadily at an object even though the head is constantly moving. This is possible because a sense organ in the ear transmits impulses to the brain which then transmits impulses to the external eye muscles.
(a) *Name the sense organ in the ear which detects the smallest head movements.*
(b) *What part of the brain receives and transmits these impulses?*
(c) *Name* **one** *substance or activity that can upset this delicate mechanism.* (AEB)

In this type of question conciseness is important.

224 Biology

3 Structured questions These are intermediate between a short answer question and an essay. The questions are usually in several parts. No guidance on length of answer is given and you should be guided by the mark allocation.

(a) *List two chemical elements other than carbon, hydrogen, oxygen and nitrogen which are required by both green plants and mammals.* [2]
(b) *For each of the elements you have chosen give **one** reason why it is required (i) in green plants, and (ii) in mammals.* [2]
(c) *Choose **one** of the elements from your list and describe how you would carry out a controlled experiment to show that it is essential for the normal development of a green plant.* [6]
(d) *In what form and by what processes are mineral elements taken up by the roots of a plant?* [2]
(e) *Explain how the nitrogen of plant protein is changed, after the death of the plant, into a form which other plants can use.* [5] (JMB)

4 Essay questions The traditional type of examination question. It is important that a plan is drawn up for these questions. This should be made on the examination paper and crossed out by a single line. The plan should list the main points and order in which they will appear in the answer. Answers must be concise, written in good English, and facts should be relevant to the question and presented in a logical order. Keep your sentences short. Remember the examiner is looking for correct biological facts and not complex sentence construction. This is not an English language examination.

Write a brief essay on the importance of respiration in plants and animals.

(CAM)

5 Practical questions These are designed to test your ability to follow instructions, make accurate observations and produce valid conclusions. Follow all instructions carefully and when asked to record your observations include all detail, e.g. size, shape, colour, smell, etc. Drawings should be accurate representations of the specimens, and you should follow all the advice given on how to draw on p226. Marks can only be given for information you provide on the answer sheet. Answers must therefore be precise and detailed. Conclusions should be made on the basis of your observations and practical and theoretical knowledge acquired during the course. The following practical work is often set: drawing and labelling half flowers, fruits, seeds, bulbs, corms, rhizomes, twigs, bones, teeth, insects and other small invertebrates; food tests, simple experiments including osmosis and observation of behaviour in small invertebrates.

Terms used in examinations

The following is a list of terms commonly used in examination questions. In each case a brief explanation is given of how you should answer this type of question.

1 **Annotated diagram** – make a large labelled diagram and beside each label give a brief description of the part and what it does, e.g.

   *By means of annotated drawings only, describe two of the following: (a) a **named** rhizome, [5], (b) a **named** tuber, [5], (c) a **named** bulb, [5], (d) a **named** corm [5]* (O & C)

2 **Compare** – state the similarities and differences between the two or more topics given in the question, e.g.

   Compare the functions of the skin of a mammal with those of the outer layers of a green leaf. [10] (O & C)

3 **Contrast** – state the differences between two or more subjects, e.g.

   Contrast the actions of nerves and hormones in coordination in a mammal. [10] (O & C)

4 **Compare and contrast** – state point by point the similarities and differences between two or more subjects, e.g.

   Compare and contrast gas exchange in a named insect and a named fish. (O & C)

   One way of planning an answer to this type of question is to list the main features of the process and state the similarities and differences shown by each named example, i.e.

Point	*Insect*	*Fish*
environment	terrestrial	aquatic
exchange surface	tracheole	gill
properties of surface	thin, moist, etc.	thin, moist, etc.

   The following type of question is helpful since it gives the points for you to consider.

Compare and contrast a named herbaceous plant with a named mammal under the following headings:
(a) maintenance of rigidity [6]
(b) nutrition [8]
(c) response to stimuli [6]   (O & C)

5 **Describe** – state in words (using diagrams where appropriate) the main points of the topic you are asked to describe. This is the most straightforward type of examination question and requires you to relate knowledge to the examiner. Answers should be concise and logically presented.

Describe how the rates of photosynthesis and respiration of a given plant may vary during a 24-hour period.   (JMB)

6 **Diagrams** – may form the basis of a question or be used to illustrate a point in another type of question. In all cases diagrams must be large, fully labelled and have a title. They should be drawn as simple pencil lines and labelled with pencil or pen. Never sketch and avoid colouring and shading. Labelling lines and arrows must touch the structure and should be neatly arranged around the diagram. They must not cross. A diagram represents a simplified or idealized representation, whereas drawings are (usually) made directly from the object and appear in practical questions. Drawings must show correct proportions.

Make a large labelled diagram of a vertical section through the mammalian skin. [6]   (O)

7 **Discuss** – give a critical account of all the points involved in the topic being written about, and their relative importance. You should make a list of all these in the plan and present them in an orderly way in your essay. This type of question has not appeared in O level examinations in the past 3 years but it may do in the future.

8 **Distinguish between** – state the differences between the subjects mentioned in the question and their implications. Give a named example to illustrate your answer.

Distinguish between pollination and fertilization.   (CAM)

9 **Explain** – state all the details which affect the subject and enable it to be clearly understood. Clarity in your answers is required, e.g.

Explain how the nitrogen of plant protein is changed, after the death of the plant, into a form which other plants can use. (JMB)

10 **Graph** – these questions may involve the construction of a graph or interpretation of presented data.
  (a) Graphs should always be drawn in pencil on graph paper.
  (b) The graph should fit the middle of the paper.
  (c) The horizontal x-axis should represent the variable which is under the control of the experimenter, e.g. time, temperature.
  (d) The vertical y-axis should represent the variable being investigated, e.g. length changes, weight changes.
  (e) Axes must be labelled, equal intervals marked and the units stated, e.g. 0, 2, 4, 6, 8, ... Time (minutes).
  (f) Points should be clearly marked either with a ⊙ or ×.
  (g) Points should be joined either with a smooth curve or straight lines drawn with a ruler.
  (h) The graph should have a title, 'Graph of . . . . .'

How to read a graph If asked to determine a value on the x-axis corresponding to a value on the y-axis, draw a line from that point parallel to the x-axis. Where it cuts the line on the graph draw a line down to the x-axis and parallel to the y-axis. Where this line cuts the x-axis read off the value.

If asked to interpret the graph, relate the changes shown by it to the biological situation illustrated. Remember that the steeper the slope, the faster the change.

11 **Illustrated account** – diagrams should be used as much as possible in the answer. These may be annotated, flow or structural diagrams. Writing should only be used to explain points which cannot be made in other ways.

Give an illustrated account of the life-cycle of either a named insect or a named amphibian. (LOND)

12 **List** – write down the facts as briefly as possible. Each fact should be numbered 1, 2, 3, etc.

  1 *List the living and non-living components of a well-balanced soil.* [10] (LOND)
  2 *List **three** requirements for spore germination.* [3] (SCE)

The Exam Boards

The addresses given below are those from which copies of syllabuses and past examination papers may be ordered. The abbreviations (AEB, etc) are those used in this book to identify actual questions.

Associated Examining Board, (AEB)
Wellington House,
Aldershot, Hants GU11 1BQ

University of Cambridge Local Examintaions Syndicate, (CAM)
Syndicate Buildings, 17 Harvey Road,
Cambridge CB1 2EU

Joint Matriculation Board,
(Agent) John Sherratt and Son Ltd, (JMB)
78 Park Road,
Altrincham, Cheshire WA14 5QQ

University of London School Examinations Department, (LOND)
66-72 Gower Street,
London WC1E 6EE

Northern Ireland Schools Examination Council, (NI)
Examinations Office,
Beechill House,
Beechill Road,
Belfast BT8 4RS

Oxford Delegacy of Local Examinations, (O)
Ewert Place,
Summertown,
Oxford OX2 7BZ

Oxford and Cambridge Schools Examination Board, (O & C)
10 Trumpington Street,
Cambridge CB2 1QB

Scottish Certificate of Education Examining Board, (SCE)
(Agent) Robert Gibson and Sons, Ltd,
17 Fitzroy Place,
Glasgow G3 7SF

Southern Universities Joint Board, (SU)
Cotham Road, Bristol BS6 6DD

Welsh Joint Education Committee, (W)
245 Western Avenue,
Cardiff CF5 2YX

Index

absorption of digested food 38, 46, 55–6
active transport 13, 28, 31–2, 92, 99–100, 108
adenosine triphosphate (ATP) 66
adrenal cortex and adrenal medulla 137
adrenaline 137, 138
aerobic respiration 65–7
  compared with anaerobic respiration 69
agriculture 207–8, 212
air
  pollution 213
  in soil 204
alimentary canal
  herbivore 56–7
  human 51–6, 57–8
allele 184, 187
alveoli 75, 77–8
amino acids
  in human nutrition,
    digestion and absorption 50, 55, 56
    reabsorption of waste 104, 108
  in nitrogen cycle 203
  in plant
    synthesis 33
    transport 94
  structure and importance 33
Amoeba, single cell animal 17, 30, 85
  excretion 105
  osmoregualtion 110–11
  reproduction 158
  respiration 71
Amphibia see frog
anaerobic respiration 67–8
  compared with aerobic respiration 69
anatomy evidence for evolution 197
anther 169, 170
antibodies 87, 88, 93, 94
antidiuretic hormone (ADH) 111, 137
anus 52
apical meristem 177
appendix 52, 56, 57
aquatic respiration 71
arteries 90–1
asexual reproduction 158–60
assimilation of digested food 38, 46, 56
association centre of brain 129
autotrophic nutrition 38, 39–45
auxin 121, 177

back cross 189
bacteria
  characteristics of 158, 214–15
  disease producing 85, 215–16
  defence against 86, 88, 93–4
  in soil and nitrogen cycle 202, 206 208, 215, 218

232 Index

balance, sense of 135
behaviour (animal response) *see* response
bile, bile pigment 52, 57, 58, 105
biological control 212
biomass (pyramid of numbers) 210
biotic environment 208–10
bird
  body temperature 113
  locomotion (flight) 152–4
  reproduction 164
  vision 133
birth 169
bladder 106, 109
blood
  circulation 88–91
  composition 85–7
  function 79–80, 87, 88, 92–4, 108, 114
  groups 88, 190, 191
  sugar level 137, 138
  body heat
    production 58, 66–7
    regulation 88, 105, 111–16
Bowman's capsule 106–7, 108
brain 128–29
breathing 75–6
see also ventilation
bronchi, bronchioles 75
buccal cavity (mouth) 51, 52, 75
budding (asexual reproduction) 158
buds 25–6
bulb 159, 160

caecum 52, 56, 57
cambium 20, 24, 178
capillaries 90–2, 107–8, 111, 113–15
capillarity 200
carbohydrates
  in animal nutrition 49, 50
  in carbon cycle 202
  in plants 32, 39–44, 94

see also cellulose, glucose, glycogen, starch and sugars
carbon cycle 201–2
carbon dioxide
  in animal and plant respiration
  see gas exchange
  in carbon cycle 201–2
  in plant photosynthesis
  see photosynthesis
  waste product 105, 109
cardiac cycle 89–90
carpels 169, 170
cell, animal and plant
  activity 28–31, 65, 71, 85
  division *see* meiosis, and mitosis
  structure 13, 15–18
  types of animal 19
    differentiation 18
    single cell *see* Protozoa
  types of plant 19–21
    differentiation and function 22–7, 31, 154, 178
cellulose 20, 25, 57
central nervous system (CNS) 125–8
cerebellum, cerebrum 128–9
chlorenchyma 20
chlorophyll 26, 39–44
chloroplasts 18, 26–7, 40
chromosomes 16, 186–7, 194
circulatory system 85
  human 88–91
clinostat 124
clone, cloning 185, 195
coleoptile response 122–4
collecting duct 107, 108
collenchyma 24, 154
colon 52, 56
colour blindness 193
conditioned reflex 127
conjugation (sexual reproduction) 162
conservation 213–14
consumers in ecosystem 200, 208–9

contractile vacuole 17, 110–11
convoluted tubules 107, 108, 111
coordination 121, 139
  see also nervous system, and endocrine system
copulation 168
cork 20, 178
corpus luteum 166–7
cortex of kidney 106
crops 207, 212
crustacean eye 133
cytoplasm 13, 15

Darwin, Darwin's theory of evolution 195–6
deamination 104
defaecation 56
deoxyribonucleic acid (DNA) 184, 186, 196
dermis of skin 111, 112
diabetes mellitus 109
diaphragm 74, 75, 76
diffusion process 28–9, 63, 70, 85
  in animals 92, 105
  in plants 99
  see also gas exchange
digestion 38, 46
digestive system, human 49–56
diploid 162, 184, 187
disease
  bacteria producing 215–16
  body protection against 87, 88, 93, 94
  chemotherapy treatment of 216
  protozoa producing 217
dominant gene 184, 185
  incomplete 189–90
dormancy of seeds and buds 201
drugs
  causing mutation 194
  treatment of disease 216
duodenum 52, 55

ear 133–5

earthworm
  gas exchange 74
  hibernation 163
  hydrostatic skeleton 145
  in soil 206–7
ecology, ecosystem 200–14
effector 120, 121
egestion 38, 46, 52, 56
embryo, human 168
embryology evidence for evolution 197
endocrine system 136–7
endoplasmic reticulum 16
endoskeleton 145, 146
energy, source and production 32, 63–4
  conservation 214
  flow in food chain 208–10
  in living processes 14, 49, 57, 66, 99–100, 108, 114, 149
environment 200–14
  body function in *see* homeostasis
  genetics and evolution related to 193, 194, 196, 197
enzymes 13, 33–4
  in digestion 9, 32, 46, 51–5
  in respiration (glucose breakdown) 65
  in seed germination 175
epidermis
  animal (skin) 71, 74, 111, 112
  plant 20, 25
epiglottis 54, 74, 75
erector pili muscle 111, 112
etiolation 123, 177
evolution 195
  evidence for 196–7
  theory of 195–6
excretion 14, 103–4
  animal 104–9
  plant 109–10
exoskeleton 145–6, 150
expiration 63, 73, 76
eye 130–3

F_1 and F_2 generation 184, 185, 188, 189, 190
fats 33
  chemical test for 51
  in human body 49, 50, 57, 93, 94, 113, 115
  plant manufacture 33, 44
feathers 115, 154
feed back 136, 138
feeding mechanisms 46–8
fermentation 63, 68
fertilization 157, 162
  in animals 163–9
  in plants 171
fish
  filter feeding 46
  gill gas exchange 72
  locomotion (swimming) 151
  reproduction 163
  uric acid excretion 104
flight 152–4
flower structure 169, 170
flowering plant
  gas exchange 80–3
  growth 177–9
  hermaphrodite 163
  sexual reproduction 169–72
  vegetative reproduction 158–9
foetus, human 168
food
  chain and web 45, 200, 208–9
  human requirement 50, 58
  plant manufacture 32
  preservation 216–17
  see also nutrition
fossil evidence for evolution 197
freshwater food web 209
frog
  gas exchange 74
  locomotion 151
  reproduction 163
fruit 157
  dispersal 172–4
  formation 172

fungi 206, 216
  see also mould

Galapagos Islands, isolation of species 197
gall bladder 52, 55, 57
gametes 157, 160
  flowering plants 169
  human 164–6
  in Mendelian genetics 185–6, 187
  production (meiosis) 161
gas exchange
  animal 71–80
  cell 69–71
  plant 80–3
  tissue 79–80
gene 184, 187
genetics 185–95, 197
genotype 184, 197
genotypic variation 193
geographical distribution evidence for evolution 197
geotropism 124
germination, seed 157, 174–6
  tropism experiments 122–4
gestation 169
gills 71, 72–3
glands 120, 135, 136–9
glomerulus 107
glucose,
  animal energy supply 57, 65, 68–9
    hormone control 137–8
    kidney reabsorption 108, 109
    liver control 57
  plant
    production see photosynthesis
    respiration and use 67–8, 175
    transport 94, 100
glycogen, animal energy supply 57
goose flesh' 115
growth 14, 158, 176–7
  animal 179–80
    hormone 137

plant 22, 121–2, 177–9
  hormone 121, 177
guard cells 27, 95, 98–9

habitat 200
  see also aquatic, freshwater, terrestrial
haemoglobin, oxyhaemoglobin 79–80, 87, 105
haemophilia 192, 194
hair, mammalian 115
hair follicle 111, 112
haploid 157, 161, 184
hearing 133–5
heart, mammalian 88–90
heat, body *see* body heat
herbicides 212
herbivore feeding and digestion 45, 48, 56
heredity 185–95
hermaphrodite 157, 163
heterotrophic nutrition 38
  see also holozoic, parasitic and saprophytic nutrition
heterozygous chromosomes 184, 187
hibernation 74
holozoic nutrition 38, 45–58
homeostasis 103, 120, 121
  blood function 88
  liver function 57
  see also body heat
homoiothermic animals 66, 113
homologous chromosomes 184, 187, 190, 192
homozygous chromosomes 184, 187
hormone 120
  elimination by kidney 109
  production 136
  sex 166–8
  summary 137
  see also antidiuretic hormone, auxin, and insulin

humus 205, 206
Hydra
  cell differentiation 18
  cell transport 85
  feeding 46
  reproduction 158, 163
  respiration 70
hyperthermia 115
hypothalamus 128, 113–14
hypothermia 115

ileum 52, 55–6
immunity, immunization 94
industrial melanism 196
industrialization 213
ingestion 38, 46
insect
  disease spread by 217
  feeding mouthparts 46–8
  gas exchange 71–2
  growth and metamorphosis 178, 179
  joints 150–1, 152
  resistance to pesticides 196
  skeleton 145–6
  uric acid exretion 104, 105
  vision 133
inspiration 63, 73, 76
instinctive behaviour 141
insulation, heat 115
insulin 57, 109, 137
ions 99
irritability 14, 120

joints
  and muscular activity 150
  types and structure 148

keratin 112
kidney, mammalian 105–9, 111
kinesis 120, 140

larynx 54, 74, 75

leaf
  fall 110
  structure and function 26–7
  transpiration 94, 98–9
learning 127–8
lenticels 82, 83
light, environmental feature 201, 208
  animal
    eye response to 131
    formation of vitamin D 116
  plant
    gas exchange 80, 81
    growth 177
    response to (phototropism) 122–3
    water loss 99
lignin 20, 21
limbs 147, 148
linkage of genes 184
liver, human 52, 57–8, 105
living organism characteristics 8–9, 14
locomotion 145, 151–6
loop of Henle 107, 108
lungs, human 71, 74–8, 105
lymph and lymphatic system, mammalian 92
lymphocytes 86, 88, 93, 94

Malpighian layer 111, 112
Malpighian tubules 105
mammal
  excretion 105
  growth 180
  locomotion 152
  nutrition 48–9
  see also man
man
  blood transport and circulation 85–94
  in environment 211–14
  gas exchange 74–9
  nutrition and digestion 49–58
  reproduction 164–9
medulla of kidney 106
medulla oblongata of brain 128
meiosis 161, 186, 195
Mendel, Mendelian genetics 185, 187–8
menstrual cycle 165, 166
metabolic rate 63, 66
metabolism 103
metamorphosis 158, 164, 179–80
microbiology 214–18
  see also bacteria, mould and yeast
mineral particles in soil 203
mineral salts
  in animal (mammalian) nutrition 50, 108
  plant uptake and transport 44–5, 94, 99–100
  in soil 205
mitochondria 15, 16, 66
mitosis 158
Morgan, Morgan's chromosome theory of heredity 186
mould
  reproduction 158, 161, 163
  saprophytic nutrition 58–9
mouth (buccal cavity) 51, 52, 75
movement 14, 145
  animal and plant 139–41
  see also locomotion, and tropism
muscle
  anaerobic respiration 68–9
  cells 19
  nerve coordinating 135, 136
  structure and mechanism 145, 149–51
  in locomotion 151–4
  voluntary 145
mutation 185, 194, 196

natural selection 185, 196, 197
nephron (uriniferous tubule) 106–7, 111

nerve cell (neurone) and mechanism 125–7
 in muscle 149
nervous system, mammalian 125–36
nitrogen cycle 202–3, 208, 215
nitrogenous waste
 absent in plants 109
 animal 104, 105
nuclear membrane 15, 16
nucleus 13, 15, 16, 17, 186
nutrient cycles in environment 201
nutrition 14, 38
 animal nutrition (heterotrophic) 38
  holozoic 38, 45–58
  parasitic 38, 39, 59–60
  saprophytic 38, 39, 58–9
 plant
  autotrophic 38, 39–45
  parasitic 215–16, 127
  saprophytic 215, 216, 217
  symbiotic 217

oesophagus 52, 54
ommatidium 133
operculum, opercular cavity 72–3
organ and organelle 13
organism 13
osmosis 13, 29–31, 85
 osmoregulation 108, 110–11
ovary
 flowering plant 170
 human 164
  producing hormone 137, 166, 167
ovule, flowering plant 171
ovum, human 165–6

pancreas, pancreatic juice 52, 55
 islets of Langerhans 137
parasite, parasitism 38, 39, 59–60, 215, 217
parenchyma 20, 24, 154
pathogens 85, 215–16

body defence against 86, 88, 93–4
pectoral and pelvic girdles 147
perennation 157, 160, 177
peristalsis 54, 56
pesticides 212
pharynx 52, 54, 74, 75
phenotype 184, 187
phenotypic variation 193
phloem 20–4, 94, 100
 secondary 178
photosynthesis
 basis of food production 32, 63–4, 202–3, 208
 materials and mechanism 26–7, 32, 39–44
 and respiration 63–4, 80–2, 109
photoperiodisin 200, 201
phototropism 122–3
pituitary gland producing hormone 111, 128, 136–8, 167
placenta 168, 169
plasma 30, 58, 85, 93
plasmalemma 13, 16, 110
platelets 87
poikilothermic animals 113
pollination 157, 169, 171
pollution 200, 213
population 210
potometer 98
predation 209–11
pregnancy 168, 169
producer, in ecosystem 200, 208–9
protein
 chemical test for 51
 in chromosomes 186
 in human nutrition 50, 104
 synthesis in plants 33, 44, 109, 202–3, 208
 see also amino acid, plasma, nitrogen cycle
protoplasm 13, 14–5
Protozoa
 causing disease 217

Protozoa – contd.
  excretion 104–5
  gas exchange 71
  osmoregulation 110–11
  see also Amoeba
pyramid of numbers (biomass) 210

radioactive carbon experiments 43, 100
radioactivity causing mutation 194
receptor 120, 121, 129
recessive gene 184, 185
rectum 52, 56
recycling materials 214
red blood cells (erythrocyte) 30, 58, 86
reflex arc, reflex action 120, 126, 127, 141
reproduction 14, 157, 158
  asexual 158–60
  sexual
    animal 160–9
    flowering plant 169–76
reptile
  body temperature 113
  uric acid excretion 104
respiration 14, 63
  aerobic 65–7
  mammal, diagram of 10–11
  anaerobic 67–9
  energy/heat production by 63–4, 114
  see also gas exchange
response 121
  animal/plant compared 139
  animal (behaviour) 139–41
  see also endocrine system, nervous system
  plant 121–4
rhizome 159, 160
rib and sternum 146, 174–5
ribosomes 16
ringing experiment 100

root
  structure and function 21–3, 25
  uptake of mineral salts 99–100
  uptake of water 97–9
roughage 50
ruminants 57

saliva 51, 52–3
salts *see* mineral salts
saprophyte, saprophytic nutrition 38, 39, 58–9, 216, 217
sclerenchyma (fibres) 20, 24, 154
sebaceous glands 111, 112
sebum 112
seed 157
  formation, dispersal, germination 172–6
selective reabsorption 103, 108
sense cells and organs (receptors) 113, 129–35
sex determination in mammals 191–2
sex-linked genes 184, 192–3
sexual reproduction
  animal 163–4
  human 164–9, 174
  hermaphrodite 157, 163
  plant 162–3
  flowering 169–74
  reduction division mechanism 160–2
shivering 115
shoot
  growth 177
  structure and function 23–6
sight 131–3
  defects 132
single cell
  animal 17
  see also Amoeba, Protozoa
  plant 18
skeleton, function and types 145–6
  human 146–8

skin
  earthworm gas exchange 74
  mammalian structure and function 105, 111–16, 129
skull 146
smell receptors 129–30
soil
  constituents and fertility 203–4
  pollution 213
species 185
  formation 196, 197
  variation 193–5
sperm, human 164–5, 166
spinal cord 128
spiracles 71, 72
Spirogyra
  cell structure and mechanism 18, 85
  reproduction 158, 162
spore 157, 158, 161
stamens 169, 170
starch
  chemical test 51, 53
  stored in photosynthesis 40, 41, 42
stigma 169, 170
stimuli 121
stomach
  human 52, 54
  ruminant
stomata and guard cells 27, 82, 94, 95, 98–9
sugars
  produced in photosynthesis 39,
  test for reducing 51
  see also glucose, glycogen
sweat glands 111, 112–13
sweating 105, 112, 114, 115
swimming (fish locomotion) 151
symbiosis 200, 217–18
synapse 120, 125, 127

tapeworm 59–60, 163
taste receptors 130
taxis 120, 139
teeth, mammalian 48–9
temperature
  feature of environment 177, 201
  regulation in animals 88, 105, 111–16
terrestrial, life mechanism 71, 108
testis 164, 165
  hormone 137, 167
thalamus 128
thoracic cavity 74, 75
thyroid gland 137
thyroxine 137, 138
tissue 13, 19
  structure
    animal 19
    plant 19–28
  see also growth
tissue fluid 92, 93
tonsils 93
trachea 74, 75
tracheoles, gas exchange surface
translocation 85, 94
transpiration 85, 94–7
transport 85
  active 13, 28, 31–2, 92, 99, 108
  in animals 85–94
  in plants 94–102
trees 160, 178
tropism 120, 122–4
trypanosoma (sleeping sickness) 217
tuber 159, 160
turgor 154
twins 195

ultra-filtration 103, 108
urea, uric acid 104, 105
ureta 106
urethra 106, 109
urinary system 106, 108–9
urine 108, 109
uterus 165
  producing hormone 167

vaccination 94
variation of species 193–5
vascular tissue of plants
  cell types 20, 21
  root 22–3
  shoot 24
  transport by 94–100
  see also phloem, xylem
vasodilation and vasoconstriction
    114–15
vector 200
veins 90–1
vegetative propogation 158–60
ventilation 63, 72, 74
ventricle
  brain 128
  heart 89
vertebrae, vertebral column 145,
    146–7
villi 55–6, 93
viruses 216
vision 131–3
  defects 132
vitamins 33, 44, 50, 58, 116

waste products
  animals 104–9
  plants 109–10
water
  feature of environment 201, 202
  pollution 213
  in soil 204, 205–6
  fundamental to living cells
    28–31, 85, 202
  in animal functions 50, 104, 105,
    108, 111
  in plant functions 45, 94–9, 109,
    154
whales 115
white blood cells (leucocytes) 86–7,
    88
woodlice response to environment
    140–1
woody tissue 20, 178

xylem 20–4, 94–100, 154
  secondary 178

yeast fermentation 68

zygospore, zygote 157, 161, 162